UFOs

The Physical and Psychic Phenomenon

Virgilio Sánchez-Ocejo

MUC PRODUCTION
2013

UFOs
The Physical and Psychic Phenomenon

Copyright © 2013 by Virgilio Sanchez-Ocejo

ISBN: 9781492932666

First Printing: 2013
Covert Art by: **Likemagickgraphics**

Library of Congress Cataloging-in-Publication Data

Printed in the USA
MUC PRODUCTION
2013

DEDICATION

Dr. J. Allen Hynek   Photo: Author
(May 1, 1910 – April 27, 1985)

*"When the solution to the UFO puzzle comes, I think it
will prove not to be just a step in the march of science,
but a mighty and unexpected quantum jump"*

Dr. J. Allen Hynek

Table of Contents

About the Author

Virgilio Sanchez-Ocejo was born in Havana, Cuba, in 1936. He began his studies at the school of La Salle, graduating later with a baccalaureate from the Institute of Havana. He became interested in the UFO phenomenon in 1956, when he saw his first UFO while studying at the University of Havana. In 1960, he moved to the United States. In 1963, he enlisted in the US Army in a voluntary program for Cubans at Fort Jackson, South Carolina. He has written numerous articles on UFOs, in English and in Spanish, for journals and magazines in the US, Spain, and Latin America. He has participated in various radio and television programs as an expert on UFOs, both in Spanish and English. For over two years, he produced the local Miami radio program, Looking for a Response, where he collected data from UFO sightings by Cuban immigrants. In 2006, he acted as associate producer and consultant, appearing on television documentaries, which were translated, to different languages, such as A Search for Chupacabras by the network BNN TV in the Netherlands, Chupacabras on Animal Planet TV, It is Real? Chupacabras by National Geographic TV, and The Strangest UFO Stories of all Time – Alien Vampire Chronicles by the Discovery TV channel viewed by millions around the world. In 1974, he traveled to Mexico for the first World Ufology Conference in Acapulco, where he met Doctor J. Allen Hynek- adviser to the US Air Force for over 20 years. He was appointed representative for CUFOS South America by Dr. Hynek, whom he traveled with to Argentina, Brazil, and Canada as an associate and interpreter. He and Dr. Hynek investigated numerous reports of UFOs and cases of abductions, as well as participated in several conventions, in those countries until Dr. Hynek's death in 1986. He also participated as a partner for project UNICAT, a UFO databank created by Dr. Hynek and later led by Dr. Willy Smith until his death in 2006. MUFON and CUFOS appointed him as Special Representative for all South America, and he was also a member of the now dissolved organizations A.P.R.O and N.I.C.A.P. In 1984, the ANDROMEDA organization of Seville, Spain awarded him a diploma as "Honorary Member" for his prominent record in the fields of Parapsychology, Allied Branches, General Science and merit made in other areas. Also, in 2006 he was named host of the Museum of Discovery and Science exhibit "Alien: Worlds of Possibilities" in Fort Lauderdale, Florida. His first book UFO, Contact from Undersea was published in 1982 by Wendelle C. Stevens. He is director of the MIAMI UFO CENTER, a non-profit organization registered in the State of Florida in 1976. Its main objectives include processing and disclosing reports of UFOs, and to discover the essence of the UFO phenomenon.

EMAIL: virgiliosanchezocejo@gmail.com

FOREWORD

*"Psychology also has not only the right
but also the duty to do what we most
shed light on this dark issue."*
                                        Carl C. Jung

My work for many years has been to try to
identify the Unidentified Flying Objects or UFOs,
so far, I have not been kidnapped by one of them,
nor have I have seen one closer. I have talked to
hundreds of people who claim to have had those
experiences. The first thing is to find a logical
explanation of the phenomenon. But not
everything that glitters is a UFO. A large
percentage of the reported cases are not.

During my research I have come across with the
Goodyear Zeppelin, small airplanes carrying neon
advertising signs in their wings, stars, comets,
NASA rockets out of course... But not all my
research is only for UFOs. My interest in UFOs
began one afternoon of the year 1956. I was
walking at the Habana University when I saw
others students looking skywards. Also, I did it.
What I saw was a series of cumulus clouds and
beneath them a bright light. I did not pay much
attention and went on my way. The next day I

read in a newspaper the following headline: "Flying Saucer over Havana", this triggered my interest in the phenomenon.

..·l raro objeto se acercaba a vertiginosa velocidad. Parecía que se iba a estrellar contra el monumento, pero de repente se detuvo y retrocedió, desapareciendo tras una estela de humo azulado...

PLATILLOS VOLADORES EN LA HABANA

(FLYNG SAUCERS IN HAVANA)

Since then, I am looking for an answer to that light. It took more than 65 years, when I got my hands on a photo taken by photographer Zayas, on May 17, 1956 of an Unidentified Flying Object hovering Marti's Monument in the Republic Square (now Revolution Square) at the side of the Havana University, published in the journal "Gente" in an article titled 'Flying Saucers in Havana". It may also be an extension of the object, according to the writer. The article said that they heard the voice of the photographer Zayas who cried: "There, there are the Flying Saucers!" While

8

pointing his camera to the sky, he shoots one picture. According to the reporter, initially it seemed a dark spot in the distance. Suddenly, at breakneck speed, the UFO directly descended at Jose Marti's Monument. In a moment, it was coming down very fast. When the violent impact seemed imminent, the strange object, which could be, identified as a small sphere flattened at both ends, stopped and backed away with a trail of blue smoke. Then it disappeared over the horizon.

My interests, in the UFOs phenomenon, started in 1974, in the United States, I begin, by becoming a member of different organizations -APRO, CUFOS, NICAP and MUFON- devoted to the study of UFOs. I saw to my delight that the most important organizations had professionals, at that time, dedicated to the study of these phenomena. Not like in Cuba, which became fashionable were Flying Saucers, was taken as jokes. In 1956, a well known beer company builds a Flying Saucer in a park. It attracts the media and hundreds of peoples from different provinces. It was surrounded by police and fire fighters and every time they tried to get close a smoke and a strange sound scared them away. The second day, the police storm it an out came a well known showgirl dressed like a "Martian". This was the inspiration of a song writer to produce a song with this lyric: "The Martians already arrived... and they came dancing Cha Cha Cha ..." In 1974, I went to Mexico to the First Word UFO Congress in Acapulco.

Researchers, from all over the world participated. It was there where I met Dr. Joseph Allen Hynek, UFO consultant for 20 years in the U.S. Air Force. I also met other important researches and even astronauts interested in these phenomena. Then, I start taking more time; not only collecting cases, but investigates it in person. Thus initiate my organization, the Miami UFO Center, which more than creates members, collects data. For more than eight years, we travel accompanying Dr. Hynek around South America after his death y 1986. He was my teacher, and I learned, from him, how to do field investigation, to evaluate reports, etc... Hynek taught me that the UFO phenomenon had two aspects: one physicist; the ship, and the other the psychic; the impact it leaves on the witnesses and the paranormal phenomena associated with UFOs. I make use of my law studies. I listened to different opinions from the witnesses of the phenomena, like a judge who hears all parties, and then, I come out to conclusions. One of the important things is to look for physical evidence left by the phenomenon; either aircrafts or their crews, and interviewing witnesses. One of these investigations gave me fame among UFO's scholars. My investigation went to Japan in the form of a documentary. This is what happened, on January 3, 1979, to Filiberto Cardenas, a resident of our community. He was in his car with a friend family on a street in Hialeah, when their car broke down, and he and his friend went out to see what happened, a powerful light struck of him, and to

10

the astonishment of his friend, he disappeared from the place. He was found 16 miles away from his abduction. The news appeared in all the press. It took me two years to investigate the case, with the assistant of Dr. Hynek, and write a book on it. But among the cases we have studied, one of my favorites is the young man who was a deaf-mute by accident and had a strange encounter. He said he was riding a horse through a field, in Florida Blanca, Colombia; and saw a "boy" standing next to him and in the field, a round object. That "boy" communicated with him telepathically and with sign language. The "boy" said eight words. We publicly talked this case, so far, not a single person was able to decipher the message. If the reader finds out, let me know!

Now retired, I have prepared this book as a legacy of my research, with a series of the most important cases, personal experiences, anecdotes, including some unknown sightings in Cuba. The city of Miami has been growing over with migrants from Central and South America, therefore, becoming a Capital of the America in the United States. In other words, the source of UFO experiences from the ones that immigrate to the U.S.A.

Chapter One

Argentina

RICARDO'S SAGA

 One of the most exciting cases, Hollywood style, in which we were involved, was Ricardo's case. Not only was the story itself was interesting, but also the circumstances surrounding it. It all began in April, 1982, when Argentine forces invaded and occupied the Falkland Islands or Islas Malvinas, a group of 200 islands, population 2121. The two largest islands are East Falkland Island and West Falkland Island (including an adjacent small island); they are a British dependency, located in the South Atlantic Ocean, east of the Strait of Magellan and northeast of the southern tip of South America. Geological, the Falkland Islands are a part of Patagonia in Argentina, being connected with the mainland by a raised submarine plateau. Under a 1985 constitution, the islands are administered by a British governor.

Negotiations to settle the sovereignty dispute between Argentina and Great Britain began in the mid-1960s at the United Nations. The talks were still in progress in April, 1982, when Argentine forces invaded and occupied the islands for about ten weeks in an attempt to settle the issue by force. They were defeated by a British task force and formally surrendered on June 14, 1982. Argentina continued to claim the islands; the British government refused to participate in further negotiations, but the two nations resumed diplomatic relations in 1990.

In June of that year 1982, two months after the Argentine forces invaded the Falkland Islands; we were visited by our friend Atilio Spinello from Mendoza, which is a city in western Argentina, located at the eastern end of the highway and railroad which across the Andes Mountains into Chile.

Previously he had called me long distance to inform me that he had a very interesting UFO case, but he would like to discuss it only in person and not by phone. It was my first impression that something strange was going on since he always talked freely with me.

When Atilio came, he explained that this man, Ricardo, had an encounter with extraterrestrial entities and was told during his abduction, just before the Falkland Islands crisis happened that the Argentine military would invade and later lose the war against the British.

Atilio said, "The problem is that after the war, some Argentine intelligence agencies were looking to interrogate him, because knowing how ended the war ahead of time, made Ricardo suspected of being a British spy. One intelligence agency took Ricardo into custody and later, after interrogating and torturing him, let him free, but with bruises and a broken arm. Right now, I have Ricardo, posing as a worker, in disguise, in my house at Potrerillo, a mountainous winter resort on the outskirts, in Mendoza. He wants to talk to you, Dr. Allen Hynek and Dr. Willy Smith".

That year we were invited to the F.A.E.C.E. Symposium in December; but due to the anti-American feeling in Argentina because our government had helped the British during the war, supplying them with military intelligence data from our satellites, relations between the two countries were cold; and we were afraid to appear publicly in front of a group that resented Americans. Atilio assured me that such was not the case. We had been there before sharing UFO information and politics was not our topic.

On the other hand, Atilio said that he had cleared our visit with an intelligence agency from the Green House, the equivalent of the White House, and was assured that no other intelligence agency could interfere with our investigation. At that time, there were 6 independent intelligence agencies in the government. Nevertheless, I placed a call to Mr. Eduardo Ficarotti, at that time F.A.E.C.E. president, and he assured me that we would not have any problem at the Symposium that the organizers were aware of that and they would take measures in that respect, never leaving us alone. Immediately we got in touch with Dr. Hynek and Dr. Willy Smith, explaining the circumstances and asking if they would still want to make the trip. Following their affirmation, we departed for Argentina on December 5.

After one and a half days of flying, we arrived at Potrerillo about 11:00 PM. We were unpacking when someone knocked at the door. Atilio answered and a well-dressed lady came in. We were introduced and after that she departed. We asked Atilio, who was she? And he answered, that she was the wife of the Green House intelligence agency director and he was in the car outside. He sent her to verify that we were all there because they had information about another Dr. Smith arriving in another city. They also left with us an armed agent named Marcelo who, by the way, accompanied us all the time until our return to the US.

From left to right: Dr. Willy Smith, Author, Ricardo and Dr. Hynek (taking notes)

We decided to interview Ricardo the next day, outside on the house patio under a canopy. After breakfast we went outside with Ricardo to listen to his experience. Suddenly, we saw an armed Navy helicopter flying at a very low altitude. Dr. Smith got his camera to photograph it but I advised him, under the circumstances, not to do it. That morning, and during the next two days of Ricardo's interview, we could observe some men in blue uniforms on the hills that surround the house. Atilio informed us that they were from the Navy and probably watching us because there was no Navy airfield or base in the area. Marcelo assured us we should not worry because they, the Navy, knew he was there to protect us and they, the Navy, could do nothing while he was with us.

Let me mention, that Marcelo also took part in Ricardo's investigation taking notes and asking questions. Aside, Marcelo turned out to be a great chef at the barbecue!

THE EXPERIENCE

Born in Mendoza, Argentina, Ricardo Jesus Velazquez, (his full name) was a professional soccer player and a part-time bricklayer. On January 23, 1981 at 8:00 PM, while jogging up and down a small rock hill, 30 or 40 meters high, which he and other soccer players used to stay in physical shape, he was confronted by two "persons". He described them as small, thin but muscular, with a dark suit like a karate uniform, and a normal head with chestnut-colored hair. "They were standing, floating some 30 centimeters (12 inches) from the ground at the bottom of the hill where there are some bushes", he said. Ricardo was running down the hill very fast and almost collided with them. "One of the entities fired a light at me, like a laser beam, just before I could crash into them; this stopped me and caused some burning in my body. Then, they spun around to leave. I began to shout insulting words at them. At that moment, they turned around and said the insults were not necessary and I should not become agitated. Then they asked me if I wanted to know why they were there and if I would like to go with them. This conversation was telepathic. They do not talk but I could hear their words in my brain", Ricardo said. "They stood beside me and then we began sliding, not walking; they did not move their hands or feet. I was also sliding between them without moving my legs. Going around another hill I could see a very concentrated light floating in the air close to the ground. We approached the light and entered it. Inside there was another light, when we passed through the second light we entered an oval room illuminated by a clear yellow haze. In front of me was a big screen, like a big car windshield. In front of it was a seat but it was floating in the air (it had no stand), with a cushion the same color as the room. There were 4 more entities with us, males; I did not see any female there. One entity on my right, one on my left and the others two in front of me. The one at my right didn't do anything; the other three were busy at the controls of some kind of machines. In total, six entities were in that room. The machines looked like drawing tables full of controls with on-and-off colored lights", he said. "Then, I started hearing a high-pitched buzz. We started moving. On the big screen in front of me appeared the outside grounds. We traveled between hills. I could recognize places; it went around 'Tupungato' city, a place that alpinists call 'La Laguna Azul' (the Blue Lagoon), the dikes 'Fria' and 'Maure', the 'Chagra' zone, etc. After that, we went up to the Andes mountain chain", he declared.

The Andes mountain chain of South America is one of the greatest mountain systems of the world. It runs parallel with the Pacific coast from Cape Horn to Panama in Central America. In Argentina the land rises in the direction of the mountains, while all the mountains ascend highly.

Earthquakes have lifted parts of the Andes over 5,000 feet during the past 20 million years. Uspallata Pass, between Mendoza and Santiago, Chile, is 12,795 feet high, very narrow and steep; it is as a whole very dangerous. The Andes have many volcanoes. Llullaillaco (22,057 Ft)) is on the border of Argentina and Chile. Aconcagua (22,831 Ft), in Argentina, is the highest mountain in the western hemisphere. The mineral riches of the Andes are gold, silver, copper, platinum, mercury, lead, iron ore, petroleum and sulfur. This gives you a general idea of where Ricardo was taken.

"I could not estimate the speed we were traveling because there was no vibration inside. I felt a force holding me, they never touched me. We made a half turn and I saw a typical rocky mountain. There we made an angle and faced the mountain. One of the entities moved to another machine and the buzzing sound became louder. I could see through the windshield in front of me that we were going to crash against the mountain but at the moment of impact, it opened like a hole without form. After going through the opening, I felt a door closing at my back. I calculate we had traveled 250 or 300 kilometers in two minutes. The light went off for two or three seconds and then we were inside a hangar illuminated by the same yellow light. Taking into consideration the 2 or 3 seconds without light, this hangar could be located 4 or 5 kilometers deep inside the mountain. We exited from the light, the same form we had entered, with two entities at my side. The one at my right, which looked in charge, went through a wall; there were no doors at the hangar. We followed, two or three meters behind him, through walls like you go through doors. We didn't walk, we slid in. We went directly through openings in the walls but without seeing one. In the first room we saw 10 entities working at machines like computers or televisions with different images. They were dressed the same. In the second room was the same but with some 15 more entities.

I looked at their screens and could see a farmer, on another screen a horse, on another a big city similar to New York because I had seen it in movies and on television, on another screen Buenos Aires. The third room was identical but with different images on their screens. We entered the fourth room; this one was bigger with only one big screen, 6 x 6 meters, and you could view it in three dimensions.

"The entities in front of me stopped at the controls of a device and mentally asked me if I would like to see the past, present or the future and learn things. I agreed but, of course, they knew my answer. They showed me a suburb with regular people: some slim, some fat, some tall, some small, dark skin, white skin, etc., some walking, some on bicycles, ladies watering the lawn, many plants, flowers but there were no cars. Everything looked quiet and peaceful. The entity at the controls looked at me with a kind of smile. Then they displayed on the big 3-D screen an empty city with perfect buildings; I believed it was Atlantis. At that moment, he asked me if I wanted to know where I came from. I answered, from my parents, my grandparents, etc. No, he said. He asked me if I really wanted to know where my soul came from. It sounded like I was not my parents son and he wanted to show me who I really was. The figure of Jesus Christ popped up on the screen, an emissary assigned by them or by the 'Father'. They used the word 'Father' instead of God. He was preaching on top of a hill, to a group of people. At the end only 8 people followed him, 7 men and a woman. They explained to me that the same could happen to me while I related my experience. I understood that although I speak to a thousand, only a few will understand me. Everything they showed me on that big 3-D screen came with an explanation. How the Earth was created from the Catholic point of view, I guess they knew I was Catholic. Then the Earth today with its ecology destroyed. They said a word I never heard before, 'Eclosica'. It was a lesson on how we are destroying the environment. They indicated the cause of man's self-destruction: the wars in Libya, Israel and later Argentina. The South Pole with snow, icebergs and warships, airplanes, soldiers fighting. It was so natural that I could perceive the smell of gunpowder, the dead. Very life like. Men could change all this, they explained. It is in our hands to do it. They displayed man-made modern arms and how absurd they are.

"There were few races in this Universe. They displayed 4 or 5 races that lived parallel. One was older than Atlantis. They called it 'Lamar'; it belonged to another cycle. They lived in tunnels, with exits at the poles. They also utilized a molecular system to create a 'hole' in rocks; therefore the sunlight could enter the tunnels. This race was similar to one that lived on Mars. There was a civil war in Atlantis when the Earth's poles switched and mountains became seas and vice versa, ending that civilization. I asked them what we could do. They answered they could reveal the way but we - humans - had to do the job.

"That was the end of my first encounter. They asked where I wanted to be left off. I thought, in the same place we met. We made the same circle. I left the light with the same 2 entities. They proceeded to re-enter the light. I ran to my home some 6 kilometers away. Everything happened in one hour.

"Nine months later, in November of that year, I was walking at night, to my brother-in-law's home, when I saw a little light close to the ground. It became bigger and it materialized into an entity. The same type as before -dark suit, etc. By telepathy he said we would have another encounter soon. The entity transformed again into a light and disappeared".

SECOND ENCOUNTER

"On January 23, 1982, exactly a year after of my first encounter, I was running, training for a soccer game, when I encountered them in the same place for the second time. They took me to the same underground hangar but this time they showed me again, on the big 3-D screen, only the South Pole: the snow, icebergs, the battles, etc. It was then that I realized it was the Las Malvinas war. They displayed warships, helicopters, warplanes, the fight, and prisoners, all of the war. At the same time they explained it was all a political issue, more business than war.

23

"Our return from their underground base was different. Their mountain is located close to a hydroelectric dike. We came out from under the dike through the water. This time they left me close to my home, some 4 kilometers away. When I reached home, I felt very sick physically and mentally. I had two brothers in the Army. I was confused and did not know what to do. Then someone advised me to consider the ufologist Faruk Allen, formerly Mendoza's F.A.E.C.E. representative".

Faruk reported that Ricardo went to see him on February 10, 1982, and it took Faruk one week to calm him down. He proceeded to record Ricardo's experience on a cassette, making a few copies and sending one to another ufologist, Pedro Romaniuk. For reasons unknown to Faruk, Romaniuk sent his cassette copy to the Argentine Armed Forces. "The Army Secret Service started interrogating Ricardo and everyone close to him. This happened in February and the war started in April. There had been rumors of a confrontation between the two nations, and the Army Secret Service believed, at the time, there had been a leak of intelligence information. I was fortunate they missed me", Faruk said.

HIGHLIGHT OF THE INTERVIEW

These are some of our questions answered by Ricardo:

Hynek: Substantially the message is that we would have to do something for the world.

Ricardo: These intelligences told me that there are key figures in this process. During our discussion with Faruk, 3 names came out: you, Virgilio Sanchez-Ocejo and Willy Smith. Could it be you?

Hynek: That really raised the whole question for me of whether I had that sort of importance. Would I be the logical person for them to contact?

Ricardo: I'll have to ask them. They had tried mentally contact with the key person but he turned them off. Why did you do it?

Hynek: Maybe I did not realize it. I went through three phases; at the beginning I thought there was something. Second, as a scientist, I had to have a foundation. And third, when I made it public. I never had a contact phase. Are they physical or non physical?

Ricardo: Yes, for me, they are physical. They are between 1.85 and 1.90 meters high, and I saw only one woman with them. They materialize and dematerialize because they manipulate the molecular structure of matter. All contactees had a common physical element. There are others that can be affected by their energy. Their suits are for their protection against that energy, and also the suits can produce an energy which they used to move humans up and down, in and out of the light.

Hynek: We could do all that, is in our hands, if their position is solid. But how do we know, if we notify the authorities, they will not pull the rug out from under us?

Willy Smith: Not everything they said has to be truth; the contact can be a test to see what you do with that knowledge.

On November 7, 1989, I went back to Mendoza, and while doing a documentary called "Door to the Unknown" (Puerta a lo Desconocido) for Atilio Spinello Video Production, we had the opportunity to examine Ricardo one more time. This time we were able to locate the mountain where he was taken by the entities, and we filmed the interview there. He did not change his abduction story; he remained bound to his 8-year-old experience.

Like Filiberto Cárdenas predictions, Ricardo's experience shows us that these entities are somehow able to know the future. We were always looking for some physical evidence, like nuts and bolts from their craft. Maybe they have nuts and bolts, but to learn from them how to know our future not only will be a great knowledge but also could be the optimal weapon. Modern science explores a universe that reveals surprises and is less adjusted to our consciousness. Psychology today falls well behind compared to other sciences.

Once Dr. Hynek pointed out:

"A characteristic of the UFO phenomenon is that it is presented highly isolated in both space and in time; it appears and then disappears".

We know that time and space is the same thing. One cannot exist without the other. Obviously, "space-time" is an important key to the UFO phenomenon, and undoubtedly it will be our next scientific evolution.

Chapter Two

Colombia

WILLIAM ORTI'Z CASE

William Ortiz

It all started one day when someone knocked at my door, when I opened it, standing there were two gentlemen. One of the two had a large built and an intense look about him. The other one had a medium size built, with bright eyes and smiling face. "My name is Larry Warren (fictitious name), and this is William Ortiz, we have an appointment with Dr. Allen Hynek at this address."Is Dr. Hynek here?" the large man said: "Yes, come in" I answer, "he had been waiting for you." Both gentlemen went inside my home and were direct them to the living room where Dr. Hynek was he was attending to the last details of our trip to Argentina, to which we would leave late that night. Leaving them alone, I went back to my bedroom to finish my packing.

I remember that, on November 6, 1980, I received a hand written letter from Dr. Hynek enclosing a letter that William Ortiz had claimed to have had three UFO encounters. In that letter, he expressed that his hearing was temporally restored during the time of his encounter and that he also had some pictures that he wanted to share with Dr. Hynek. In the letter, Hynek ask me where we should meet Mr. Ortiz, at the airport or in my home. I thought since I would like to see Mr. Ortiz's photographs, why not use my home as a meeting place, since we had 10 hours from Hynek's arrival to the time we have to leave on our trip to Argentina. I answered Dr. Hynek's letter advising him that he should use my home as a meeting place since we had time to spare before leaving to the airport.

We were invited to travel to Argentina by F.A.E.C.E. (which stand: Argentina Federation for the Extraterrestrial Science Studies). The Federation, at that time, was formed by 320 groups. They organized their first International Symposium, which was held on December 6, 7, and 8, 1980 in the city of Mendoza. F.A.E.C.E. wanted me to extend a personal invitation to Dr. Hynek knowing that I met him at the First World UFO Symposium in Acapulco, Mexico in 1977. Also, in 1979 Dr. Hynek joined our Miami UFO Center team in the Filiberto Cardenas abduction case. The F.A.E.C.E. wanted us to share with them the Cardenas case, and in return they would share with us their investigations of others UFO phenomenon in South America.

Suddenly, I heard Dr. Hynek calling me to the living room. "Virgilio" he said, "Mr. Ortiz experienced an encounter that would be a very time consuming investigation, and since you live in the area, I think you would be the perfect candidate to handle this investigation. That is of course if you want to take on this investigation". Without a hesitation, I agreed and promise keep him posted. Then I asked Larry Warren his phone number to help me set up a time and place to start investigating Mr. Ortiz encounter. By the way, Mr. Warren never answers my phone calls, and I never see him again. It was Mr. Ortiz the one who show up at my home unexpectedly for the next two years.

THE EXPERIENCE BEGINS

In 1950 at the age of 13, Ortiz was riding his horse on a gravel road in his parent's premises a little past 7.p.m. on a clear day. When peering through the growth of vegetation on one side of the road, he noticed a child but continued on his way. Then in an opening through the weeds and in the top of a rock, he saw a disc and children around it. After clearing his eyes, he realized that these were not children but part of the UFO crew. He stopped in confusion, looked over his shoulder at the child next to him and realized that it was no child, but a crew member. Looking closely at the entity, he noticed that the clothing was some type of uniform, very tight to the body and covering the neck and legs, and boots. The collar ended like a turtle neck, and he could see something like a symbol in the form of a V on the shoulders. The hands had only four fingers, or maybe five, he was not really sure. The alien's hairless head was much bigger than the rest of his body.

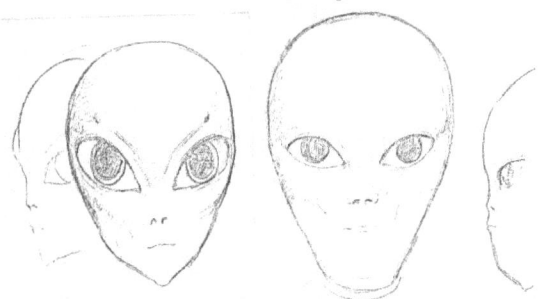

The eyes were big, oval shaped and very black, even though some crew member's eyes were smaller than others. There were no ears, just a little hole on each side of the head. The nose was small as well as the lips, which never moved. The skin color was a grayish brown. The entity in front of him appeared to be a male. The other crew members looked the same, even though they were 100 feet away. At this point, Mr. Ortiz was concentrating on the entity that was 6 or 7 feet away. This entity, knowing that Ortiz was aware of what was taking place, looked directly into Ortiz's eyes and started sending him messages, and Ortiz clearly heard these messages in his brain and at the same time the alien was using hand language.

There were eight words in the message:

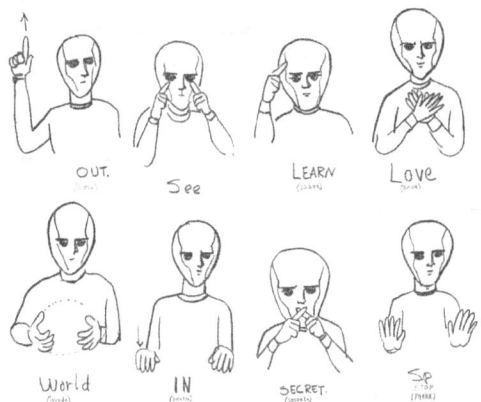

OUT. See LEARN Love

World IN SECRET Sp

"IN", "WORLD", "STOP", "SECRET", "OUT or SKY", "SEE", "LEARN", "LOVE". Ortiz could not remember the sequence of the words because it happened too fast. Ortiz doesn't know what the entity was trying to tell him. After the message, the entity made a turn toward the rock. At this moment, Ortiz could not see the rest of the crew. The entity went back to the UFO, half walking, half floating, very fast. Then the UFO went straight up, makes a turn to the southwest and

disappeared into the horizon. Ortiz, in his astonishment, did not even notice his surroundings or the reaction of his horse. All Ortiz could think have been the impact of this on his life, now and in time to come.

THE GREAT ROCK

33

At the beginning of his experience, Ortiz saw a UFO hovering over a big rock and entities were surrounding the rock, the local people now call it "The Great Rock". The rock measures some thirty feet in diameter by twelve feet in height. Ortiz calculated that the UFO was of the same size as the rock. This rock is located on a piece of land, an acre in size, and next to this rock there is a house. The rock has drawings engraved in various forms: lines, circles, disk shapes, serpents, and unknown symbols and figures.

Though people from Ortiz's town believed that the engraved symbols were done by the Indians years ago, Ortiz believed that the entities were the ones who engraved the symbols in the rock, thousands of years ago.

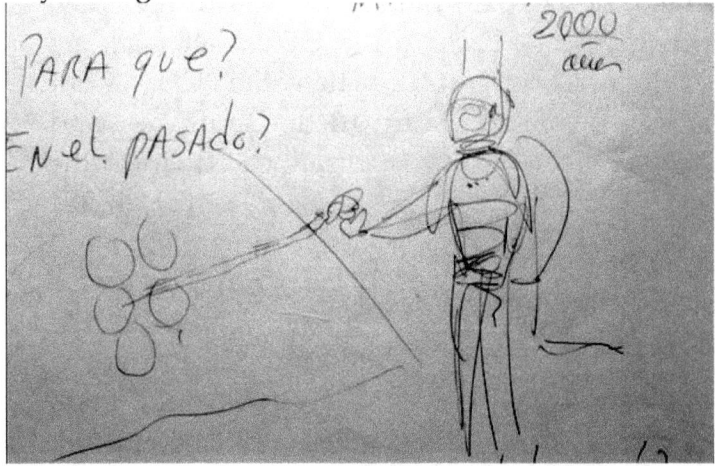

The engraving or carving on the rock goes back to prehistoric time before the invention of writing. To this day such engraved rocks remain due to their indestructibility, like paper.

The study of these engraved rocks suggests that human occupation existed more than 2,000 years ago. Studies even show that rocks had been engraved before mankind began. It is difficult to interpret the engraving on these rocks. The so-called Great Rock is not an exception as others engraved rocks are in Peru, in the ruins of the Inca civilization, Machu Picchu, Cuzco, Marcahuasi, Sacsayhuaman, Brazil, and Central America in the Yucatan Peninsula, Mexico and as well in North America. Many of the megaliths in Central America are engraved with geometric designs; one pattern that is frequently seen uses the disk and circle shapes. The disks or circles engraved in the Great Rock symbolize the Sun.

For some modern psychologists, like the late Dr. C. G. Jung, the round object, whether it is a disk or a circle also known as the "mandala", symbolizes the encompassing which is intended to protect and defend against outside influences. Dr. Jung stated that some historical and psychological knowledge shows that the circular symbols have played an important role in every time period.

On the Great Rock, we also found engraving of serpents. The serpent is likewise a very ancient symbol. In Mexico, the God Quetzalcoatl is represented by a feathered serpent, whose image

35

decorates much of pre-Columbian art. Quetzalcoatl was the major deity of Teotihuacan and all subsequent Mexican Indian civilization. Here, in the United States, we have the Great Serpent Mound, build by the Adena Indians; its coils are almost a quarter of a mile long along a ridge in southern Ohio. The Great Serpent Mound can only be viewed from the sky. Some scholars could not accept that these monuments and carvings had been created by the ancestors of the Indians.

Serpents have been used as symbols on the entities' uniforms. In the early morning hours of December 3, 1967, Patrolman Herbert Schirmer of Ashland, Nebraska, had an encounter with UFO entities that had, on the left side of the chest, an emblem of a winged serpent.

In the Cardenas case, during the second encounter his wife, Iris, reported that: "On the entity's suit, on the right side of the chest, they had an emblem of a serpent in the form of an 'S'." William Herrmann of South Carolina reported being abducted in 1978 by humanoids and that the beings he saw had a metallic figure of a wiggle serpent worked into the fabric on the left side of the chest on their one piece jumpsuits.

The Great Rock engravings continue to be a mystery; some local people believe that the Great Rock functions as a radio nuclear beacon used by the UFO. As the population of this area grows, the rock is now surrounded by houses.

WITNESS

Close to this place lived Mr. Jose Morales Gomez, and with a notarizing document he asserts: "In the last month of 1948, at approximately 9 a.m., I saw a UFO make three circles, to an altitude of three thousand meters, on top of the Great Rock. The rock has engraved in high relief with several rockets with different sections and also several flying saucers of different sizes. Upon making the three circles, the UFO geared toward the southwest, without any noise.

"In the middle of the year 1955, at midnight and arriving at my home, I saw the lights of a UFO at the same height as the previous one, and without any noise, it made three circles over the rock, taking three  minutes to make each circle, then it went to the southwest."

On November 3, 1975, at 8 p.m., I was returning home from work, when 5 children, who were playing in front of my house, indicated a large light, making circles in the top of the rock. My ten year old daughter Martha came running and asked me if it would be a satellite launched by the United States. I observed it and compared it with those I had seen previously in the same place. I told the children that we were watching a Flying Saucer that it could not be a satellite; at that moment the children interrupted me responding; 'because a satellite has an orbit and does not make circles, as the light we are seeing.' At that moment my daughter felt fear and grabbed me by my hand asking: 'Papa, can the Flying Saucer hurt us?' I looked at her and answered, 'Don't worry, I have seen them before two different times and they have not hurt anyone."

"From my home to the mentioned rock is two hundred and fifty meters and from rock to the principal park of Floridablanca is seventy meters. Therefore, by what I had seen and by the drawings in the rock, I speculated that when this region was not inhabited, Flying Saucers landed here and recorded in the rock the figures of rockets and ships in which they traveled."

"These Flying Saucers are powered by nuclear energy, and this region is recognized by the Colombian Mining Inventory as very rich in uranium; I think that their ships came here to carry the uranium. As of today, they continue using the rock as a flying reference or beacon, to guide their flights. Always after making three circles at the rock, they change course and continue to travel southwest. I also think that, at the rock, they buried a nuclear battery to give them signals, when they fly over it. It serves them as a beacon to direct their flights."

This is part of the legal document signed by Mr. Jose Morales Gomez. From him, we learned the amount of sightings that have taken place. Also, he witnessed from a different place the same UFO that contacted Mr. Ortiz. His opinion about the rock and the UFOs are open. At present, we are following reports of sightings from the rock at Floridablanca.

SIGN LANGUAGE

Ortiz was 13 years old when he communicated with the entity in Spanish language. When we met he was 45 years old, having leave most of his life in this country and learn the words in English, his new language. I had to double check and translate the entity's exact words with him; you can see it in the sketches, at the bottom of the English word that Ortiz wrote. Also, we have to understand that sign language does not exist for every word in English or Spanish and that some signs have been changed and updated during that time. We know that the words Ortiz received in his brain were in Spanish, and he insists they were spoken words, not thoughts. Now, we question if the hand sign communication with Ortiz would be in Spanish or English? We find out that every country has developed its own system, which has been standardized to some extent within that country. Although it's true that today's sign language has crossed national barriers and permits communication between deaf persons of many countries, and also is being used to cross the language barrier with speaking people. Today American Sign Language is considered to be the most refined and complete sign systems in the world. This make us think that the sign language used with Ortiz, by the entity, was their very own system, and the words were transmitted by voice into Ortiz's brain to make sure he understood it. So we have come to the conclusion that there are handicapped entities. We are now approaching something that was ignored by ufology. These entities, whatever they are, are not perfect creations. So they have entities that are born with normal hearing or sight but in whom the sense of hearing or sight become nonfunctional later through lack of use the developing of telepathy as a mean of communication, even though some entities could be born with deafness or blindness from genetic causes.

Ufologists have to be prepared to get all the information in cases like Ortiz's. We found out that there were no sign for words like: UFO, Sighting, Abduction, etc.; sometimes we used finger spelling with Ortiz. Finger spelling is the use of hand position to represent the letters of the alphabet; there are 26 different single-hand positions representing the 26 letters of the alphabet; it is a historical element of manual communication, used by the monks of the middle Ages. It was not easy to work with Ortiz, but I found out that deaf people are patient with you when you do not understand them but also, you will have to be patient with yourself. I encourage to improvement of American Sign Language vocabulary by adding words used to describe the UFO phenomenon. Having experiences denoted with the true sign language in that way, it would be easier for deaf people to explain them and easier for us to understand.

ASTRAL THEATER

Ortiz's experienced is not the only one that has happened to a deaf-mute person. During that time, I was scheduled to give a lecture about different UFO topics in a small theater, in a shopping center, the Astral Theater had two hundred seats. In one of my topics, of course, I included Ortiz's case. I put an ad in a local Spanish newspaper, "Diario de las Americas". After two hours of presentation including questions and answers, I was still collecting my things, when my wife came running and told me to go to the lobby of the theater. Going past people, I found Ortiz, whom I had not seen for a few months, communicating with five other deaf-mutes. At the beginning, I thought that they were Ortiz's friends whom he had invited to my lecture, so I went to

41

find out what was going on. People were still surrounding us, when the manager of the theater came and very polite, asked us to leave because it was late and he had to close the theater. We moved to the shopping center parking lot and continued there.

I became aware that these deaf-mutes who came to my lecture had never met each other; they went to the lecture because they read the ad in the paper that mentioned a contact of a deaf-mute person with an extraterrestrial; they sat for two hours looking at the slides but not knowing what was going on, or did they? In the lobby, they recognized Ortiz and wanted him to explain his experience. They also told us that they had had UFO sightings, and they had been trying to explain their experiences with little or no luck at all.

DEAF-MUTE ENTITIES?

The William Ortiz case opened a door in the study of ufology. For some time, we asked ourselves why the entities did chose him, knowing that he was deaf-mute, making the communications with the hand language. From accumulating data and experiences of others abductees and contacts, there emerged a contact pattern. The sign language used with Ortiz is not exactly the one used by American Sign Language, not the one he learned in Spanish. That make us think the sign language used with Ortiz was their own system. In consequence, they are deaf-mute too!

We are dealing with congenital deaf entities. They are probably born with nonfunctional hearing, and this is why, in the abduction or contact descriptions, the ears are very small or only a hole is seen where ears should be. For that reason, they develop a very sensitive telepathic communication system. Sending and receiving through it is a very common practice among them to communicate. And like our deaf-mutes, only some guttural noises or cries can be emitted. Their mouth, for the same reason, appears to be very small or like a little line; their use of it is almost nil. In general their ears and mouth are atrophied.

Stories of deaf-mutes entities can be found in practically every abduction and contactee stories.

IMPACT ON ORTIZ

As expected, a great impact was left on Ortiz. His paintings, aside from portraits which he makes for his living, shows the influence of these entities from the origins of man to the present time and toward the future that, Ortiz thinks, will end with the creation of the cosmic man. Without needing words, Ortiz's work is projected from our ancestors toward the future of man, the same way that was expressed by many other contactees by means of words, oral or written. Apparently a mark exists, or a pattern is left in the minds of all contactees that alter their psyche, changing their way of thinking. Perhaps that change is the real purpose of these contacts. Ortiz's contact made a change in his way of thinking.

The dual nature, physical - psychic, of the phenomenon has the investigators in a quandary.

Dr. J. Allen Hynek described the dilemma of the UFOs as similar to the dilemma of theoretical physicists. Physicists are aware of the paradox of light: on one, hand, light can be conceived of as "particles"; on the other hand, light can be conceived of as "waves". Hynek argued that physicists have learned to live with the dilemma of light. "In the same vein", Hynek continued, "UFO investigators may have to learn how to live with the dilemma of UFO activity: UFOs sometimes are perceived as objects, and UFOs sometimes are perceived as psychic phenomena."

In Ortiz's case, the UFO and the entities were physical, but the contact and the message were psychic.

For Ortiz, the physical sighting means to him that he did not have a dream or hallucination. The entities appeared physical to convince Ortiz of their reality. Since the contact, Ortiz devotes much of his time to diffusing knowledge of his experience and considers the entities as "friends". Ortiz advised me that, though he did not fear them, the contact surprised him since he never imagined that something like that could happen to him and in his own town.

Ortiz's contact makes us think that these highly developed intelligent beings have some goals or purpose; beginning, preserving and increasing those contacts. Actually, we believe that there exists a specific purpose in each experience. Several reasons have been given like: rejuvenate the Earth (ecology), to impel humanity in its evolutionary development, etc. Up until now, nobody knows what exactly the real purpose is. Perhaps the entities are far from our reasoning. The evidence is sufficient to support the hypothesis that the UFO phenomenon is a huge operation, which is conducted by unknown, but sophisticated intelligences). What we still do not know is: To what point, can it change us or influence the human conscience? What are the dangers of these encounters? And if we are in danger, how can we stop them?

CHAPTER Three

Miami

FILIBERTO CARDENA'S CASE

According to Art Levine of "MIAMI NEW TIMES", the Cardenas incident is *"the most famous abduction case in Miami history"*.

From the time I began studying UFOs in 1956, I always wished that someday I could come to discover everything about the phenomenon. I never could imagine how complex and complicated this might be. Though sometimes we felt discouraged, always something would come up to renew our interest, a note in the newspaper, someone would call to tell us of their experience or they were witnesses to another sighting, or something else. These things fired anew in us sparks of returning interest. The disbelief in the unknown, the fruitless search for some real evidence, a screw, a bolt of the strange apparatus so generalized, that which we call Unidentified Flying Object.

There are many and very good arguments that makes us think that we may be being visited by intelligently controlled vehicles, piloted or not, that do not belong to this terrestrial plane, our three dimensional world. We call them extraterrestrial because they do not belong to our contemporary world. Their origin offers various possibilities: They could come from space. They could be travelers in time, or travelers from a parallel world or from another dimension. They could be a psyche phenomenon. Our personal hypothesis is that the phenomenon treats of perhaps a synthesis of all these possibilities, and perhaps even more.

Of the whole UFO phenomenon, what is more intriguing, astonishing and disconcerting are the cases of direct contact. Most of these occur unexpectedly and without notice. Also is the apparent lack of announcement by the contacted a disconcerting problem.

Here in Miami, on January 3, 1979, occurred one of the kidnappings, an abduction of a human being by a UFO. One difference in this from many others is that it presented a wealth of information. There were tests and predictions given by the aliens. Upon to now, all those who have participated in this investigation have been astonished. Finally, they accepted it as it is.

For those who investigate the phenomenon, like me, Dr. J. Allen Hynek, scientist and astronomer, former president of the center for UFO Studies (CUFOS), decease, has given us a form of classification for the distinct kind of sighting. He also provided some terms that has come into common usage:

NL._ Nocturnal Lights. Unexplained lights seen in the night sky.

DD._ Daylight Disc. Disc-shape objects seen in day light.

RV._ Radar/Visual. UFOs seen by witnesses and also painted by RADAR at the same time.

CE-I._ Close Encounter Type I. UFOs seen at more than 500 feet distance.

CE-II._ Close Encounter Type II. Physical evidence encountered at the place of the UFO contact. Marks on the ground. Broken branches, etc.

CE-III._ Close Encounter Type III. Contact of some kind with the occupants of the UFO. This is the most extraordinary of the Close Encounters. The actual sighting and contact with the beings from the UFOs.

DEFINITION. The definition of a UFO according to Dr. Hynek is the following:

"A UFO is an object or light seen in the sky or upon the land the appearance, trajectory, and general dynamic and luminescent behavior of which do not

suggest a logical, conventional explanation and which is not only mystifying to the original percipients but remains unidentified after close scrutiny of all available evidence by persons who are technically capable of making a common sense identification, if one is possible."

The UFO phenomenons decidedly contain physical aspects. It can be painted (registered) on RADAR; they emit light and sound, make marks on the ground, and break branches from trees, stop automobiles, and cause psychological traumas in animals as well as in human beings. But when a UFO case treats of a contact, it becomes isolated in a short time. One reason, is the fear that the witnesses feel of being ridiculed, fear of being ridiculed in front of their friends and family. This fear is paramount if the degree of strangeness is high. For this reason the witnesses to such a case isolate themselves. They feel confused in their experience and withdraw for fear of ridicule. This tendency to isolation is also abetted by the strangeness of the event.

It is relatively easy to inform oneself about the sightings of nocturnal lights and daylight disc. These do not expose the witness to critical judgment of his mental condition. To see a strange light in the night or a ship, apparently metallic, flying in the heights of the sky, generally does not expose the witness to ridicule. But, on the contrary, if he has seen a disc-shaped ship land with flashing lights near the patio of his house at 02:00 in the morning, and he sees small beings similar to humans, it is another thing entirely. This opens the invitation to ridicule it.

At first, some people frankly related their experiences, not only to their friends, but also to authorities. They encountered blank faces and even laughter and some of them were even persecuted as if they were possessed of the devil. Others confided in their spouses and in some intimate friends. In this case their experiences ultimately came to light after a time producing a delay in informing those interested. A sophisticated person, conscious of the reaction and the inclination to ridicule, will tell of a nocturnal light or a disc, but never an encounter of the third kind. Scientists and professionals have related their encounters with lights and discs, but they haven't reported a single case of humanoids or abduction. The curtain of ridicule effectively remains.

Today one must be endowed with valor, integrity and a high sense of responsibility to report experiencing an encounter of the third kind. He must be prepared to defend the truth of his experience, not only against ridicule, but also against skeptics and some religions. He also exposes his family to a type of attack that requires great personal honesty to endure, not only for himself but for his family as well. These conditions were faced and the responsibility was assumed by Filiberto Cardenas and his family. Thanks to them we are able to offer you this report of his experiences.

The experience of this man has been investigated by special team of professionals including engineers, doctors, psychologist, neurologist, attorneys and two professional hypnotists. Also it received the special attention of Dr. Hynek who maintained contact, and advised in difficult moments when we needed his cooperation. The mayor part of this book, concerning the whole story of the experience, has been taken directly from the four hypnotic regressions performed on Cardenas. From an editorial point of view we have arranged them to offer a chronological sequence of the experience.

Author, with Cardenas (standing) and Dr. Hynek (seated).

Dr. Hynek (seated) with Cardenas and witnesses.

Almost all of the UFO abductions have a minimum common denominator. Usually the witness only remembers having seen a UFO, and very slowly, little by little, he begins to remember having been in the present of "creatures" that are very different. The experience is normally blotted from the memory of the witness for a time. Later, by means of a dream or by vague recollections he begins to re-illuminate some details that the witness has suspected are involved in the unusual occurrence. The details of his experience almost always are found accumulated in the most profound depths of his consciousness. In the Cardenas case there were witnesses at the moment of abduction in the form of the Marti family. When

53

they reported his disappearance to authorities a state alert was imposed and a research for the missing man was begun. When he was returned two hour later he was discovered an impossible distance across the Everglades from his abduction point, in a confused and traumatic condition and was picked up by police authorities at the return site. The conditions evident produced a state of general anxiety to know what did occur. The police dedicated much time and attention interrogating everybody involved trying to verify the realities of these circumstances. Exhausted, the police investigator came to the conclusion that this must indeed have been a **Close Encounter of the Third Kind**, and to our astonishment he made this entry on the official police report under Type of Offense.

Other data that tended to corroborate what had happened was the physical marks left on the body of Mr. Cardenas. These have been described in the medical report of Jackson memorial Hospital which we have a copy of, but which for ethical and professional reasons we will not reproduce here. Also we have been asked not to publish the names of some professionals who gave time and energy to this project. My gratitude to all of those whose only interest has been the scientific investigation of a phenomenon that concerns us all equally.For those who believe in the existence of UFOs it will be easier to accept the story of what happened to Mr. Cardenas. For the minority, the skeptics, who refuse to accept the conclusions derived from our investigation, I am sure they will encounter substantial information they will find difficult to refute.

Is this experience of Mr. Cardenas real? For the moment each must draw his own conclusions. But there is no doubt that a time will come when we will know more about these CE-III cases. For now, it all seems incredible and even in part incomprehensible, but of one thing there is no doubt; the witness believes in what occurred, and I consequently do also.

Virgilio Sánchez-Ocejo
Miami, Florida.

BIOGRAPHY OF THE WITNESS

Filiberto Cardenas was born in the City of Santi Espiritu in the province of Las Villas, Cuba, on October 31, 1933, to a family of scarce resources. He began his schooling in "El Maja" school. Later, he when to "Colegio Clara Luz Farina" where he studied to the fourth grade. Later at "Colegio La Salle" he graduated from primary school. Moving with his family to Havana, Mr. Cardenas continued his education at the "Instituto de Marianao" to his third baccalaureate year. He studied physical culture and physical therapy and became an electro cardiac technician.

He enlisted in the Cuban Army in 1951. He survived the Communist revolution of Fidel Castro in 1959 with the grade of sergeant and shooting instructor. Persecuted by the new government, he was obliged to seek refuge in the mountains and from there fought until made prisoner in 1960. He carries nine bullet wounds in his body. He was imprisoned from 1961 t0 1970, a time full of incidents such as head of a hunger strike for 21 days to obtain improvements in the prison.

Freed from prison, he arranged his departure from there to the United States, where he arrived on February 6, 1973. At the beginning of his exile he dedicated two years to the exercise of his profession in massage and physical therapy at a private clinic operated by some doctors. From 1975 until the beginning of 1976, profiting by the boom in construction he worked at a number of different tasks and jobs trying to get ahead. Saving his money he bought, near the end of 1976, a gift shop and boutique business that he operated under the name of "Zarabanda Gift Shop". In September of 1979 he sold this business and bought a gasoline station in the city of Hialeah which he owned and operated during the initial investigation in this case.

THE EXPERIENCE BEGINS

On the evening of January 3, 1979, Filiberto Cardenas was in his gift shop, in Hialeah, when he received a call from his friend Fernando Marti. Fernando asked Filiberto to accompany him to the outskirts of the city to buy a pig from the local merchants, as he wanted to roast it the following Sunday. Because of the demand for pigs during the Christmas season, Fernando had not been able to get one. In a short time he appeared at Filiberto's business with his wife Mirta and their daughter Isabel, who was 13 years old.

Fernando agreed to drive his friend's station wagon after Filiberto said he was tired. With Fernando at the wheel, Filiberto in the front passenger's seat, and Mirta and Isabel seated in the back, they drove out of the city by Highway 27, also known as Okechobee Road. They drove to two farms but had no luck finding a pig for sale. Still further on, and losing patience, they saw another sign indicating a farm with pigs for sale. It was already about six o'clock in the evening. They turned off onto a side road, following an arrow that marked the desired direction, and from there they turned onto another rural road in bad condition which led to the farm. The place was operated by Mr. Jose Hernandez, who was in charge of the property. He informed them that he did not have a single pig left for sale.

Confronted with another disappointment, they decided to terminate the search and return to the city. As they came off the dirt road onto the side road, the automobile began to lose power, and the engine died. They coasted around the turn and came to a stop on the right side of the road. Mrs. Marti said that while they were checking the trouble under the hood, she would get out and cut some wild flowers that grew alongside that road. After collecting various bunches and putting them in the trunk of the car, she and Isabel got back into the automobile. From the time she got out to cut the flowers, Mrs. Marti heard a sound in the air, but nobody paid any attention to it because small aircraft are common in the area. It was well into the investigation when the witnesses remembered that they had heard the sound before the abduction also. Fernando, at the wheel, tried to start the engine but there was no response at all. He exclaimed, "What is the matter with the car?" The men looked at each other and they got out of the car. Fernando opened the hood and they both looked in trying to see what could be wrong, to locate the failure. Fernando insisted, "I can see nothing wrong with the car, but we still have no power". He returned to the seat and tried to crank the engine again. Nothing, not even the lights would function. "Anything happening?" he exclaimed. Filiberto was in front of the car looking under the hood near the battery. He didn't know much about mechanics and tried to see if the cables were loose or grounding, but they seemed to be firmly connected to the battery. Fernando got out of the car again and looked down past the hood near the windshield thinking that the problem could be in the general electrical connection situated near the steering column.

They were like this, Filiberto under the hood in front and Fernando under the hood on the right-hand side, lying over the top of the engine so as to see behind it, when suddenly both of them realized that the engine was reflecting red and violet light in sequence. At the same time they heard a strange sound. Fernando later described it as "a swarm of bees". The sound as well as the light that illuminated the engine increased, and the whole car began to shake. Mrs. Marti, who was sitting on the back seat with her daughter Isabel at her side, began to panic. The Marti family came to live in Florida from California because of a bad earthquake. This had left a profound impression on Mrs. Marti, and her first thought, upon hearing the sound and seeing the light, was that they were facing a similar phenomenon. She pulled Isabel down across the seat of the car and covered her with her body as she screamed in panic.

When Filiberto heard the shouts from Mrs. Marti and her daughter, he tried to run to their aid but felt paralyzed. He could see lights and hear sound but could not move. He felt as though something restrained and impeded his movement. Fernando, in fear, tried to crawl further under the hood, seeking protection, when he also found himself immobile with his feet sticking out in the air from under the hood. He could not move.

Filiberto ascended up in this position.

Filiberto felt as though the force that paralyzed him began to lift him and suspended him in the air. Fernando, from under the hood, could see Filiberto as he began to rise. He could hear Filiberto shout, "Don't take me... Don't take me". Filiberto could see the car as he was lifted off the ground. "I was about 3 feet above the ground when I felt like everything was becoming dark and I lost track of what was happening".

The noise and the light ceased and everything seemed to return to normal. According to the witnesses, everything; levitation, sound and light, occurred in a fraction of a second. Fernando came out from under the hood and looked toward the sky to see "like a bulky object (UFO) that ascended and then moved away". Full of fear, remembering that his wife and daughter were still in the back seat of the car, he shouted, "They have taken Filiberto...Mama, they have taken Filiberto". He got into the car and looked under the seat for something with which to defend himself, but couldn't find anything. Then he got into the driver's seat and tried to crank the engine. After several attempts the engine started but it ran very poorly, "as if it were out of gasoline". He also saw smoke coming from the engine. When he got the car running, he returned to the highway. The car little by little began to run more smoothly.

Along the way he thought he should advise the police, but he was afraid they would not believe him and would think he had done something to Filiberto. Then he decided he had to run the risk, and near the edge of town he stopped at a service station on upper 29th Street. From there he called the police, but they told him that he would have to call them back from a private number so that they could verify the call.

He then called Mrs. Cardenas and said that, "A light took Filiberto away." Mrs. Cardenas thought that he was trying to tell her that they had run a red light and had an accident and that Filiberto was injured. Fernando got back into the car and he, Mirta and Isabel continued along the road; and as they came to the town of Hialeah, they saw a police car. He stopped and explained to the sergeant in the patrol car what had just happened.

Meanwhile, Mrs. Cardenas got into another car and headed for the service station from which Fernando had called, she was looking at every corner for the supposed accident. She spotted the station wagon, along with a number of police cars that had stopped at a commercial shopping center.

There she found out what had really happened. At first, the police presumed that Filiberto would be found lost or unconscious. Fernando, in his confusion, thought that he might be mistaken about what he had seen, and decided to go back and look. Since it was already dark, the police tried to contact the Air Base at Homestead, to send an airplane or a helicopter with lights to the spot where the incident took place.

While all this was taking place, Filiberto first became aware of a sound of tires running on pavement. That was his first reaction. Then he observed some very bright white lights near him, moving. These came from a car that had almost run over him. He was in the middle of a different highway, the Tamiami Trail, later found to be some 16 kilometers south of the place where he had disappeared two hours before. He was half-unconscious, exhausted, and sweating profusely. The driver of the car got out and spoke to him in English, which he did not understand. Filiberto was crawling on his hands and knees and the driver tried to stop him. The stranger grabbed him by the jacket and dragged him toward the shoulder of the road. There he left Filiberto and made it to a telephone and called the police. He reported that he had encountered a man crawling along the median between the two lanes of the highway, and this man was in danger of being hit by a car.

The first officer to arrive on the scene was Patrolman William Christian, who at first felt he had a drunk or someone who had been assaulted and left on the highway. A second officer arrived, but they could not communicate with Filiberto because of the language barrier and also the condition that Filiberto was in. Filiberto does not speak English but is fluent in Spanish, having been raised in Cuba. They searched his pockets and found identification. They decided to take him to the police station. On the way Filiberto began to recuperate. From the identification papers found on him, the police radioed ahead to the police dispatcher a general description of what was happening.

Meanwhile, in Hialeah, the police were getting ready to go out and search for the missing man when they received his description over the radio. They suspended their search plans and took Mrs. Cardenas and Fernando and his family to the police station.

When they arrived at the station, the police had Filiberto in a room where they were interrogating him. Hialeah is a separate and distinct police jurisdiction, so the newcomers also interrogated Filiberto. It took almost an hour for the police to complete their separate interrogations. A Sergeant Sanchez came to Filiberto and gave him a card which would authorize him to get an analysis for radioactivity. According to one official, something very strange and very uncommon happened to Filiberto. On the official report, under Type of Offense, he wrote: CLOSE ENCOUNTER OF THE THIRD KIND. This may be the first time in the United States that on an official report, the police admitted that abduction by a UFO had taken place.

The group left the police station, and without exchanging words, headed for the Clinic Pasteur in Hialeah, of which Filiberto is an associate member. There in the emergency room, they were received by one of the nurses who, after hearing what had happened and seeing the police note, called the physician in charge, Dr. Fernando Grosso. When we interviewed the nurse, who prefers to remain anonymous she said: "At first, I didn't believe it, but later after carefully observing the patient, and hearing the events that had transpired, I am changing my opinion and believe that they are telling the truth. They had some type of experience. What impressed me most was the daughter. Though she didn't say anything her face reflected her fear."

Dr. Fernando Grosso told us that at first he thought that this was some drunk or perhaps a drug addict. When he came into the emergency room and saw the protagonists and the daughter, he began to find out what had occurred. They related the events and details described here Dr. Grosso told us that his interest was aroused by Fernando Marti's expression when he said; "They did not take me because I hid under the hood of the car."

Dr. Grosso told us, "I looked at them and asked, ' Are you telling me the truth or is this all a big lie?', but each one had the same story, so I came to the conclusion that it was not a lie. From the beginning Filiberto had been telling me that he felt bad. Then I took his blood pressure and it was normal. I noticed three superficial abrasions and burns, one in the middle of his forehead and the others on the sides. He was weak, and he said his legs felt very much unstable. I noted that he was a little nervous and excited. The Marti family seemed to have calmed down now. Mirta Marti told me about something like a light, very bright, that enveloped them as she screamed to Fernando and Filiberto: 'Careful...Careful...' Suddenly remembering something else, Dr. Grosso told us, "They were sent here by the police suggesting that they be tested for radioactivity. Since I could not do the test, I sent them on to Jackson Memorial Hospital." I asked him what he thought, and he replied, "I do not think it is a fraud".

The witnesses left the Clinic Pasteur and drove to Jackson Memorial Hospital. By then it was 11:30 at night. There they were met by the doctor on call, who informed them that he likewise did not have the equipment to do a radiation exposure test, however he would get in touch with Homestead Air Force Base to see if they had the necessary equipment. Later they were informed that an expert from the Air Base was on his way to the hospital to conduct the necessary tests.

Meanwhile, the doctor gave Filiberto a general examination. Filiberto felt very thirsty, and he felt as if his body were projected in front of him. They were seated in a reception room when they were informed that the hospital was receiving telephone calls from radio stations interested in talking to them. Filiberto said that he didn't want to talk about anything and he didn't want to see anybody. They were shown to a room where they were assured that they would have privacy while waiting for the technician from the Homestead Air Base to arrive. They remained there until nearly 4:30 AM when a man dressed in civilian clothes arrived with a large case.

Saying he was the technician from the Air Base, he took out an instrument from the case and commenced to pass it over Filiberto's body. In a little while he advised them that he could not find any type of radioactivity on Filiberto but that this does not necessarily mean that Filiberto was not exposed to some kind of radiation. "Many times the reaction appears after a few days," he said. The hospital recommended that Filiberto stay several days for observation but he refused. He preferred to rest at home. So it was "thumbs up" on condition that if he felt anything abnormal, or if he felt bad, he would inform them immediately. They all left the hospital at 5:00 AM Thursday, January 4, and returned once again to Hialeah to Filiberto's home.

But instead of peace and tranquility, waiting was an army of radio, television and newspaper reporters. The news had traveled like wildfire. Some had even forced doors to get into the house. "The surprise I received upon arriving home was greater than the surprise of what had happened to me."

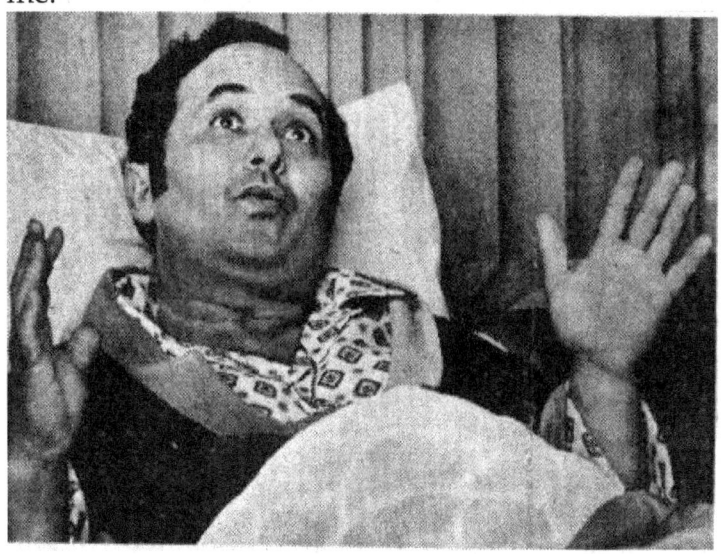

Filiberto later confessed to me. "The lights of the television crews hurt my eyes." Filiberto could only go out at night because of the pain the UFO and the television lights caused him. "I was trapped in my house," he said, referring to the reporters.

Filiberto began to experience erotic pressures and entertained sensual thoughts. He wanted to make love to his wife, and when he commenced to do so he experienced a large and prolonged orgasm. His erection was so hard that it hurt him while at the same time there seemed to be no end to his sexual appetite. Another thing that most attracted attention was the amount of water that he ingested. While he was in Jackson Hospital, he confessed, he had drunk more than 25 normal glasses of water, and in the following first days he drank water constantly, though later the anxieties of thirst began to disappear. Also in those first days, when he would lie down upon his bed, he could see through the wall, something like a figure that carried something in his hands. This manifestation lasted only seconds and he could not define what it was. Later we supposed that this was his first impression when an entity came near and placed a helmet on Filiberto's head.

In this conversation that we carried on with Filiberto, he seemed more relaxed and deliberate. When we first met him, he could not maintain conversation with the newsmen. They continually change the subject, and sometimes talked at length without stopping, or he changed the question in the middle and asked for another. He was suffering from the irritation in his eyes and it bothered his vision. Bright lights, like automobile headlights, caused him considerable discomfort. By now a week had passed with him remaining in seclusion and he still could not see clearly. The clinic found his pulse and blood pressure normal as well as his reflexes.

The marks on his body that were discovered and described by the doctor at the hospital, as well as by our own doctor, looked like floor burns or abrasions though they did not form scabs. The smaller ones on his hands and feet disappeared in a few days. I photographed those on his hands when I visit him on the 14th. They looked superficial, like bug bites. He had a large one on his forehead, two at the hairline on the sides of his forehead, one on each foot, two on his shoulders near his chest and others. He had two large ones on the muscles of his legs near his genital area. There were small marks all over his hands and feet as well as his legs, like bug bites. He also had them on the backs of his fingers.

Earlier, on Friday the 12th of January, we returned in the evening to visit Filiberto and to introduce him to the doctor who was part of our investigation team. The doctor performed a preliminary examination and made these notes:

In the days immediately following the abduction Filiberto slept very little. Only a few hours were sufficient and he did not feel tired. Also during this time he felt very active and was surprised that he did not fatigue. In the first days, he informed us; his urine had a very strong penetrating odor and was of a dark color. He could pass almost all day without taking food or drink and still did not feel tired or debilitated. He defecated normally. He confessed that he sweats heavily and that his sweat also had a strong odor as well as his whole body. He could not overcome this odor with any deodorant he tried. He tried using different kinds of soap with no more success, and he could not get rid of the smell. He said the odor smelled sulfurous. He passed the first days resting on his bed because he felt his knees weak and he was afraid he might fall. He said he felt like his lower leg, from knee to foot was separated from the rest of his body. He said this sensation began when he was in Jackson Memorial Hospital that first night. At one point, while they were waiting for the arrival of the radiation technician, he wanted to go to the bathroom, and he felt like his body was projected ahead of him and he could feel nothing from his knees to his feet. This sensation made him afraid and he continued to stay in bed most of the time. He felt changes in body temperature. At times he felt hot in his chest and cold in his feet at the same time. This sensation would not last and the temperature would change; cold in his chest and hot in his feet. At other times he felt very hot all over and would sweat with the sulfurous odor though the temperature in the house, through the central air conditioning system, remained the same. With respect to the strange sex drives, he told us that in the first days he did not seem to have any interest. His head hurt like he had hundreds of needle points pricking him, evidently produced by the helmet that the alien placed on him when he was aboard the ship. The size of the marks on his body ranged from 2 centimeters down to almost invisible.

Before terminating this preliminary examination, it was suggested that a neurological examination should be performed before we initialed any hypnotic sessions. We should be sure of his physical and mental condition and know that there are no deficiencies before we begin. A neurological examination was scheduled for Monday the 15th. After an intense neurological examination lasting three hours the neurologist pronounced the patient normal, with no deficiency, in normal mental condition, and of average intelligence. He had no detectable nervous affections.

We had to be sure that Filiberto was in good health and normal in every way before we could proceed. We knew that anyone with any defect, psychological or mental, with epilepsy for example, could imagine such abduction. In such a case a hypnotic regression might reveal a product of his epileptic condition and not a real experience. We had to be as certain as possible. We finished the physical examinations and decided to commence the hypnotic sessions on Saturday the 27th.

As he began to recover from the trauma of the initial experience, Filiberto was overcome by curiosity and felt impelled to return to the abduction site again and again. He went back there several times. He noticed that every time he went back there his watch gained a lot of time. Then on site at the abduction location he noticed that his watch was running very fast and that was making a whirring noise, which stopped as soon as he left. For some time every time he pointed his right index finger at the watch it would speed up and make the whirring noise. This incident finally diminished and went away. Several other witnesses, beside me, observed this event.

THE ABDUCTION

After having been paralyzed by a combination of mysterious light and sound Filiberto woke up in a seat that seemed to hold him in place by some kind of suction which restrained all his movements. He was in a small room. At his side were three strange figures. One of them, though of human form, seemed more like a robot. The other two also had a human appearance, and seemed to be alive. They were of small stature, a little smaller than Filiberto (who was a small man himself), and they were dressed in very tight fitting suits, contoured to the body. One of the strange beings approached carrying a special kind of helmet in his hands. He raised it and placed it on Filiberto's head. This helmet seemed to be full of small needles that came down to the shoulders. The beings tried to communicate with Filiberto, speaking in a language that sounded to Filiberto like German. When they realize that Filiberto did not understand, one of the beings rotated a button on the right side of his chest and then began to speak in English. Filiberto indicated that he did not understand that either. Again the strange being rotated the button and began this time to speak in Spanish with a Portuguese or Italian accent. Meanwhile they continued making tests on Filiberto's body these test left 108 marks on his body. In this place where they had him detained, he could not see outside, Filiberto experienced the distinct sensation of flying in air. Later he felt like the velocity was diminishing, then he felt some jerks, and a port was opened. The entities made him pass through to another bigger room. There, on a high seat, like a throne, was seated an individual wearing a cape. His body was similar to a human body. He wore a chain on his collar that fell to his abdomen, from which hung a triangular-shape stone that rotated in many directions. A bright light came from the wall, which impeded Filiberto's ability to observe closely the facial features of this alien entity. The walls of this place were in bright colors and seemed to be made of some kind of Lucite material, or perhaps like transparent resin acrylic. He found himself sitting paralyzed in the present of a robot-like entity and two others in tight fitting suits. These one, on the high seat, communicate with Filiberto in German, English and finally in Spanish, while rotating a button on the right side of his chest each time he switched language. At the beginning they used a kind of electronic devise to communicate with him while at the same time transmitting ideas telepathically.

During our hypnotic regressions I ask Filiberto:

V S-O. - Between them, what language do they speak?

Filiberto. - They talk with some sounds...

V S-O. - How do you communicate with them?

Filiberto. - It seems that they introduced something in my right ear and then, they talk to me by means of a sound.

V S-O.-Can you explain that sound?

Filiberto. - Very strange. I feel like a "Hum" sound in my brain.

During the abduction the entities place an implant in Filiberto's right ear. They told him it was a transceiver; in this way they could communicate with him in the future.The conversation revolved in turn from the subjects of human beings to humanity. On the walls they projected images, something like television pictures, that showed scenes from the past, the present, and also the future. All of this equipment was controlled by buttons that the entity had under the arm of the seat, and also on the floor in front of the seat.After this they opened another port and the captive Filiberto was carried to a small room, where he was placed in a seat similar to the first which sucked him down and impeded his movements as before. He was now in a small ship that was discharged from the mother- ship. Nearing the end of this flight, Filiberto could see what looked like a stretch of narrow beach approaching.

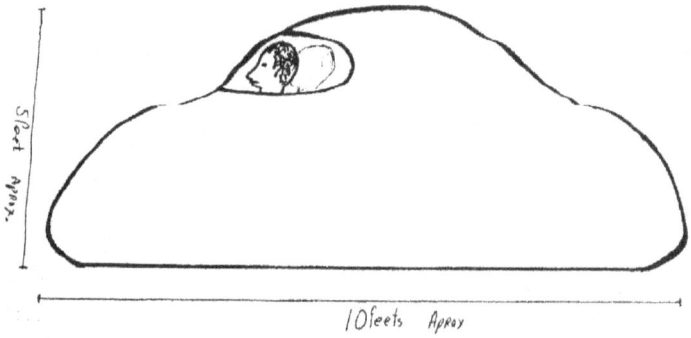

Draw of the small craft where Filiberto flew underwater.

There the entity who seemed to be the pilot of this ship disembarked from the craft and, with something he carried in his hand, made a signal toward the base of a high mountain. In this place the captive could see large rocks, some vegetation, and a "small horse." The animal was later identified as a llama. One of the rocks opened up and became like "a tunnel toward the sea." From there came other flying objects. The pilot reentered the ship carrying Filiberto and it whirled toward the sea with the others. In front of Filiberto there appeared a kind of windshield, very close to his face. The UFOs began to move and plunge into the sea. All was obscured by the incredible velocity at which the vehicle moved. The ship veered to the right and began to lose speed. In front of them Filiberto could now see a tunnel with walls that seen illuminated, as if they were phosphorescent. The ship went into this tunnel and later came to a stop in a place that was completely dry. It looked like a large cavern but he notice that it did not have any stalactites or stalagmites. It was a very big place. Here was a place made out of rock, where he noticed two symbols. One of them had the form of a serpent. It was of great size, as big as an "electric light pole." The other was similar to the first but smaller. In that place the entities disembarked from the ship with their captive and took him to a rock, where they let him sit down. They make him drink "a liquid that tasted like honey," which they told him was for nourishment. They opened an enormous door, and a number of "people" came out. Filiberto felt as if he could not breath and a pressure on his chest. The sensations and odors were very strange in this place. At this point someone came up to Filiberto and said: "WELCOME." This individual spoke to him in perfect Spanish with a South American accent. He looked like an Earth person. He informed Filiberto that he was "from Earth and had been for some time working with the entities." He also said that "he should be happy, because he was going to receive some instructions from a human being like us."

After they had taken Filiberto through another door toward a street of what seemed to be a city, they crossed it and entered a small building. In this place Filiberto felt like he was sucked up against a wall. This panel revolved a turn and converted itself into a sort of table. Paralyzed, the captive observed the ceiling, while at the same time he could see entities moving around him doing things.

At one side of the wall he could see his clothes "floating" in the air, and he now knew he was nude. They put a light in his eyes, something in his ears (which they later told him was a transceiver so they could communicate with him), and examined him with other instruments.

From the walls came mechanical arms full of instruments with which they looked at and tested most of his body. One of these arms connected something to his penis and sucked and ejaculation of semen from him. He felt no pain but he could not move because of some kind of invisible restraint. Upon terminating the examination they let him get up and get dressed again. They went down a corridor until they arrived at another room.

This place was the same, or very similar to the control room of the mother-ship. It had the same kind of high seat that rotated, an individual wearing a cape, television displays in the wall, etc... He demonstrated, by means of the televisions, to Filiberto, new and different things that were going to occur. Later he signaled to a reflection in the floor of "three triangles or pyramids united by a halo of fine light." He explained that "Those are the controls that we have here in the Earth. One control is in the Pacific Ocean (where we are now), another in the Atlantic Ocean, and the other deep inside the earth."

Another entity came up to Filiberto, and showed him another distinct place. Along the way, at times, he stopped, putting his hand on the captive's shoulder, which put him to sleep. Later he would awaken him and ask, "Are you rested," and they would continue the march. When they arrived he showed Filiberto a 'book', with many photographs of distinct places.

He made Filiberto think that this had taken those 18 months. For food he gave Filiberto "some things like pills." For a time, Filiberto felt like he was going crazy. They passed another habitation where there were two individuals "who looked like Earth people" that were all gray "like the ones they use in laboratories." He was taken to another room where there was a party going on like some kind of a reunion.

After that he was taken to a great room where there was a great ship in a vertical position "like our big rockets." They went inside of this, and encountered in this spaceship three more entities, which placed him in one of those suction seats as before, and then they set up the controls and manipulated the ship for departure.

Filiberto could see nothing of what was happening outside. After a short trip the door of the UFO opened and Filiberto was let out of the ship, in a pasture. An entity opened his mouth and made him drink something. At this time the captive began to feel bad.

The UFO took off vertically at high speed and disappeared in the sky, and Filiberto made a supreme effort to orient him. He didn't know where he was. He began to move his feet on the Earth again.

The Experience of Maria Elena

On Monday February 19, about 6:30 in the morning, Filiberto called us on the telephone. At that time I was driving on the road to work with my wife Maria Elena. When she returned home and got the message, she call back only to be informed that Filiberto was sleeping, and not to call back until after 10:30 that morning because he had spent all night out and needed to sleep. Maria Elena relates the events as follows:

"At 10:30 in the morning I called Filiberto back. He immediately informed me that they (the extraterrestrial) had said that he could bring me and other persons to the place where his abduction had taken place. He told me that in life a most important thing is LOVE and that I had been selected. He also informed me that one of my daughters would also be selected, that we should have faith. Filiberto continued the conversation talking about the sentiment of LOVE, its importance, and that I should go and meet the extraterrestrial."

"We ended the telephone conversation and I hung up. Almost immediately it rang again with Mario Rodriguez (another investigator in the case) on the line and I recount to him my conversation with Filiberto. He wanted us to get together that evening to discuss the things that were happening and coming to pass, and so we arranged it."

"There were the three of us, Mario, Virgilio and I seated in my living room speculating on what Filiberto had told me early in the morning when, at 11:30 PM, the telephone rang and it was Filiberto saying that it was now the time to go to the place."

"Mario and Virgilio began to give me instructions about what could happen or could not happen in case there was a contact and they abduct me. They didn't want to frighten me and tried to analyze everything from a logical point of view, though none of us allowed any assurance of a contact."

"After certain instructions we all went to the Cardena's home. I asked Mario and Virgilio not to get out of the car because I didn't want to risk breaking the connection or interfere with their presence. Upon entering Filiberto's house I came to realize my suspicions about who the other person would be. It appeared to be the parapsychologist Patricia Hayes. Patricia had been since the first days near Filiberto experimenting and also studying the case. Sometime later Filiberto told me that her experiments were not exactly scientific, but on the contrary speculatively bringing her students, as part of the program, to his home to receive, according to her, extraterrestrial energy, but instead receiving more delusion than anything else. From that time Patricia went away until she separated herself completely from the case. Nobody had anything to say about that."

"When we entered the house, the only thing Filiberto talked about was LOVE (in an altruistic sense) and that we should go to the encounter. At 12:00 midnight we went out to meet them. Before arriving we could see the sky through the car window. It was clear and full of stars. I studied them and thought which of them could be a UFO. Upon arriving at the entrance to the side road, Filiberto put out the lights of the auto and parked at the side of the road. There in the darkness we held hands and kissed on the cheek in a sign of LOVE. With the light out, Filiberto proceeded along the road until we arrived at the place where the first abduction occurred. Filiberto got out alone and began to walk a little behind the car. We couldn't see him in the darkness of the night but in a minute he returned to the car. Then he told us he felt that the place of the first contact was a little more ahead. He got back in the car and we continued some two blocks. We stopped again as he informed us that we had arrived at the place and we could get out. The place was well known to me, having been there in the company of Virgilio and Mario many times. Sometime we had waited until sunrise. For this reason we were not in the least afraid. What most preoccupied was the sentiment of LOVE we should have, when in reality I didn't feel any and I was more curious about what might happen. Also I didn't want to unduly influence anything. Patricia asked me if I didn't feel a certain heat at one side of the road more than the other. I answered yes but very slowly. Filiberto began to walk and got away from the rest of us, until he disappeared in the darkness. Patricia, a little nervous, asked me if I knew where Filiberto had gone, and I answered no, and we continued waiting. Some time passed and it became apparent that fear was growing in Patricia. I was amazed that I didn't feel the same thing."

"Finally Filiberto appeared in the darkness and came up to the car, and we asked him, 'Did you see anything?' He answered no, that he only had felt a little heat on one side of the road, but nothing else. Then Filiberto discovered a mark in the form of a cross that had been painted on the asphalt of the road. This mark had been made by surveyors tracing a curve at the end of the road. Filiberto asked me to stand in the middle of the cross and so I did. I don't know why but I stood erect, closed my eyes and my ears, and commenced to ask that they come and appear at that time. I was in the act of doing that when there immediately commenced to blow a strong wind that beat the trees on the other side of the road. Every moment the force of the wind increased. Soon I became afraid and opened my eyes, turned to the others and said, 'What is happening? Why is the wind so strong?' In the confusion one could see Patricia, who up to this moment had been at my side, give one jump and was standing at the side of Filiberto who was some 15 feet from me. In our faces one could see surprise and a little fear on the part of Patricia. In those seconds I didn't know whether I wanted to go toward them or remain where I was standing. Then I decided to go toward them, and I note as I walked that I felt a little seasick. I could see that my feet were not standing on the road! At first I attributed this to having smoked a cigarette, something that I do not do frequently. The calm returned again and the trees returned to stationary shadows of the night."

"Filiberto, without saying any words, returned to walking and disappeared in the darkness. In about five minutes he returned and said we should go, that nothing was going to happen. He said this in an agitated tone. I began to dispute going with Filiberto, saying that now is the time we should wait, that now was when the extraterrestrial would be likely to come. But he insisted, and we all got into the automobile. I still had the feeling that something was going to happen. We had not gone but a few meters when, looking through the window toward the shrubs, I saw some eyes that looked at me. I continued looking until I lost them in the obscurity of the distance. I didn't say anything to the others about what I had seen."

Sketch by Maria Elena of the "eyes" seen glowing in the tall scrub that grew along side of the road at that point.

"When we were, after returning, in the house of Filiberto, he called me aside and asked insistently if I had seen anything. I was afraid to tell him anything and so I denied it. Filiberto, with tears in his eyes asked me if I was telling him the truth. He judged that he had seen me, when I was standing on the cross and the wind was strong, elevated some ten inches from the road. I thought this explained the seasickness and hope I felt when I walked toward the others. But 'THE EYES'...'Really, didn't you see them?' I took a little time before I affirmed those things. Today I am sure that what happened was a very strange experience."

Days later we put Maria Elena under hypnotic regression and reviewed the whole thing that happened, confirming the above. Since she is my wife, these experiences place me in a delicate position. I don't want any of the investigation group to think that I am involved in a farce, and that my wife is also involved. For my part, I cannot think that my wife would fool me and the same for Mario Rodriguez, who for many years has investigated the UFO phenomenon as Uruguayan representative for M.U.F.O.N., an important and serious organization here in the United States. The only one who could have prepared a farce was Filiberto whom we have known for only a few days. But it all seems to indicate with witnesses, doctors' statements and police reports that he has in truth suffered an experience. I lived those moments at a time when I was pressured by friends who insisted that I should not follow this case with the objective us assuring myself that it was all a lie, that it could not be true. They obliged me continually to proceed seeking the help of international research groups to work together with us in examining the reports. In this manner I felt supported. Also, if the circumstances began to involve me also (as I hoped), there would still be other investigators to take over the investigation immediately, and I would pass over to be a new witness in this case. I always felt that the investigator should not in any way become involved in the circumstances of the case. He should remain outside the case in order to be able to make rational deductions based on the evidence without being unduly influenced. The fact that my wife Maria Elena was now involved in this case could endanger my position as an impartial investigator. But at the same time I felt that her inclusion would give me an opportunity to live, together with her, the experience itself, taking the investigation to a level of understanding that justified our inquiry on this basis.

THE SECOND ENCOUNTER

On the night of February 21, 1979, Filiberto and his wife Iris could not sleep and decided to go to the place where Filiberto was abducted. It was around

5:00 AM, when the second encounter with a UFO ship and his occupants took place.

After returning to his house, Filiberto called me and told my wife what had happened. He said that they were very tired and that he would call back again after 10:00 in the morning. They would try and get some sleep. That afternoon, I received a call from Manuel Rodriguez, Investigator of the Miami UFO Center our local group, who maintained a little distance from the Cardenas case, calling to inform me that he had received calls that people at Miami International Airport had observed a UFO that morning. Rodriguez had recorded a telephone conversation with one of the older employees at the airport, in which the employee said that about 10:00 in the morning he had observed a large mother-ship and various smaller objects flying around it. In the conversation the woman, Mrs. Julie Gonzalez, said, "I and four companions saw a large round thing like a plate very well illuminated. At first my companions saw the one. Then soon we saw two more objects come out of the large one. They were very high. I saw like a reddish ship which moved around among the other three. It had the form of a fish, elongated, without wings or a tail. The upper metallic part was brilliancy. We were in the 'satellite' of the airport and we were observing from a part near the runways. The four ships were of the same size. Then we do not know how they disappeared. We continued to observe the sky to see if they would come back into view. The sky was cloudless and very clear. We did not see anything else. The other witnesses are Ricardo Sanchez, Francisco Valdez, and the other two I don't remember their names. We all work on the morning shift." Days later we were able to obtain an address for Ricardo Sanchez and he accepted to meet with us at his house. This is how the conversation went: "I was on the rest break when my companions told me they were observing a light in the sky. But because there are many airplanes, I thought it was one of them. Then I saw that they insisted on looking toward the sky, so then I decided to look also. I could see one disc. Then I went to the other work companions, Francisco Valdez and Julie Gonzales and said that I was looking also to know what they were looking at. Our supervisor, Harold, was also with us and he too was there looking. There were five or six of us there. The object seemed fixed in the sky. It was round and had like three lights, one very white, one yellow, and the other one also white but more opaque than the first one, or you could say that it had one white light that shore brighter than the other, and also a yellow one. At the sides of the ship one could see two other ships a little smaller, of the same form but smaller. They had only one light each. It looked like one object with two more alongside it. The bright white light in the center was fixed but the yellow and the more opaque one pulsated. We watched them for twenty to thirty minutes. We got tired of looking at them."

V S-O. – Where did the UFOs were? They were in front of you? Where did you face, north... south... east... on west?

RICARDO. - I was facing west.

V S-O. - If you divide the sky like a clock with 12 directly overhead and 9 on the horizon, at what angle did you see the UFOs?

RICARDO. - The objects would be at about 10.

With these two answers we were able to localize the mother-ship with the other UFOs directly above the place where Filiberto was picked up, which is the same place where only hours before this observation, the second encounter of Filiberto and Iris had taken place. One can see that Ricardo Sanchez and the other witnesses were standing facing the contact place. If they observed the UFOs at an angle of 60 degrees they would have been situated directly over the contact point. But let us go over to the experience Iris and Filiberto Cardenas had that morning.

"The UFO appeared from behind us as we stood there. It made a turn at about 60 to 80 feet altitude above our heads, descended and hovered about a foot above the ground. We could hear a sound

90

that didn't seem like it should be coming from a ship this large. We could see that the ship had two levels or stories, the smaller level under than the larger one. It had lights around it: Blue, Violet and bright white. I (Iris) stayed in the lower level and did not see above."

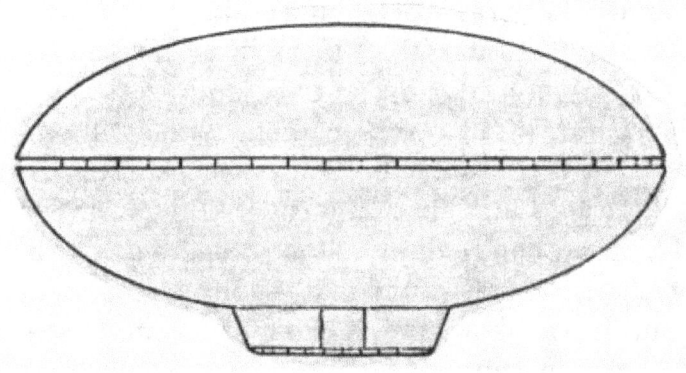

Sketch of the UFO, gondola-like, for the second trip.

"Iris saw the ship arrive. She took out a cigarette and lit it, very naturally. I told her I didn't think she should do that because they might not like it. Then she did not know what to do with the cigarette. In comparison I would say that the ship was a little larger that a truck or auto bus, though of a very distinct form. We entered (the UFO) up a ramp about eight feet long. We could see inside but nevertheless, it gave me the impression, or better, the sensation that my body passed through the body (transparent material, like glass) that was there. It was like I was going to collide with something but passed through. It was like a window of crystal, which upon passing through, we felt a distinct atmosphere, almost like we were out of this world! I felt myself floating. I felt that my body was weightlessness. My thoughts and ideas were of great intensity. When I looked back outside through the 'door', it seemed as if it were a division between two words, very distinct and separate". "Referring back to the entities, they gave me the impression that there was not much physical difference between them and us, despite the fact that I had not seen them without those suits. They all looked to be of strong constitution. I got the bright idea that they covered their whole body, head and face with something as a protection for the walking ones that surrounded us, and it was that made it difficult for me to see well their configuration."

"They were dressed in a one-piece suit of very special brilliance. It was the color of silver and reflected the lights around them. (Iris) They were not very tall. They were shorter than Filiberto and were light weight. I saw four of them one was a woman. I was aware of this because of the form of her tightly fitted suit. The suit covered her whole body, hands and feet, leaving only an aperture for the face, and it came down and covered half of the forehead. On the right side of the head where the ear should be, they were a bulge in the suit like an audio phone. (Here again, it seemed as they needed a hearing apparatus) From the neck to the bottom of the back near the buttocks, they had five thin cables or flexible transparent tubes, which did not, impelled their movement. Besides this they had other buttons and controls on the front of the suit that could be operated by the alien being."

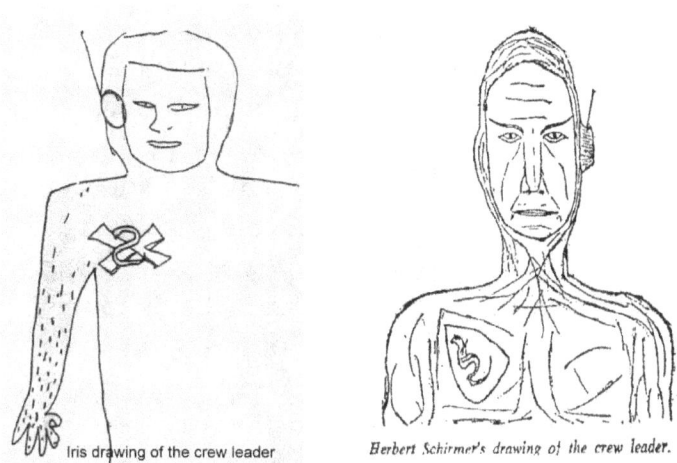

Iris drawing of the crew leader

Herbert Schirmer's drawing of the crew leader.

Iris sketch of the serpent emblem was almost the same as the sketch by Herbert Schirmer, a police man abducted on December 3, 1967.

"The face was normal, much like ours, but the eyes were elongated and had eyelashes like ours. I could not see the eyebrows. Either they were covered by the suit or they did not have any. The nose was smaller and a little flattened. The mouth was larger and long without having much lip or rather the lip was quite fine. They opened their mouth to talk but I could not hear their voice. The face ended in a small light beard."

We have to remember in their encounter Filiberto and Iris were able to remember their experience without the need of hypnosis. Filiberto and Iris confirmed that the entities resembled a deaf-mute person.

"On the suit, on the right breast, they had an emblem made up of a serpent in the form of an 'S' reversed, or maybe more like a 'Z', in yellow or orange, with rounded corners, with a wide 'X'-shaped cross lying down underneath. I could not see their hands because they were covered by the suit extending down over the fingers like a glove. No buttons, zippers or closures of any kind were seen on clothes. They sneezed constantly. (They later explained that the sneezing was caused by the presence of human beings.)"Iris Cardenas is still talking. "Inside the ship there was a sound something like that of parrots, a great number of parrots. I could hear them perfectly but I could not see them. They must have had several cages for them in this ship."

"The entities paid a great deal of attention to my painted nails, both fingers and toes. I was wearing sandals at the time. They looked at my painted nails. There was only one that spoke to me. He communicated mentally because I could not hear his voice. He spoke very delicately to me. I felt good with them, they did not frighten me. It seemed like I was floating and I felt very tranquil.

Instead of feeling afraid and wanting to run, I, on the contrary felt peace and tranquility."

"At a point I asked the one who talked to me if he would let me to touch him. I was like St. Thomas wanting to see for myself before believing and I wanted to touch him. He (the entity) said to me, yes, that I could. He raised his right arm and I could see that he had a body under the suit. The suit material seemed to have a soft scaly texture."

"In the lower level of the ship where I stayed the whole time, there was a small cabin full of televisions in rows, one alongside another, many in double banks. There was a narrow seat with a high back, as if it were for the captain of the ship. It was very prominently placed. This seat rotated. There was another seat in which nobody was sitting and they seated me there. On that floor around me there were small lights. When I sat down I observed the lights around my seat, which began to brighten in different colors. The white light to which we had become accustomed went out and I couldn't see it any more. The lights were clear and brightly transparent, such as nothing that we have here. The floor was made of a very strange material. It was not plastic, but was a smooth flat material, completely unknown to us. Also it had various levels of elevation. I didn't see any walls as such. The walls were complete covered with machines and television pictures like 'windows.' Inside the ship one had the sensation

95

of not standing on the floor, but more like floating. For the whole time I was there, some twenty minutes, I was conversing with them, but I was not talking. Not like we are now. The one who talked to me was sitting in the high seat in front of me, and as he spoke he looked at me intently. Filiberto was standing at one side on the ship then he was escorted to an upper level within the ship."

"They, the entities, walked very rapidly there inside the ship. You would see them here and then almost immediately they would go over there. The one in front of me smiled. They had a language of their own which they used to communicate between themselves. It sounded to me like they were talking in some kind of Arabic dialect. (Later she said it was like guttural sound) I did not understand them. They were very small. They smiled at me as they were saying, 'Be calm, nothing is going to happen to you.' In the conversation that I carried on with the one seated in front of me, in the high seat, he talked of love, universal love. He told me much about universal love. He said that they came on a mission to Earth and that they selected people for contact simply by accident this person was subjected to a series of tests. If that person felt love toward them, then they often continued the contact. But if, on the contrary, they did not feel any love they did not contact them again."

They allowed the contactee to say that he had seen them (the entities) without interfering with his memory. He said that they did not come to harm us as they are messengers. They told me that this is the only way they can come here to Earth, without causing fear or panic. Many for this reason have been contacted only once. If the person contacted does not feel love, or if he does not report his experience, or does not respond to the needs of others contacted, then they do not contact them. For that reason, they told me, there are here on the Earth, many have been contacted only one time and never again. But if, on the other hand, a person contacted comes to know them and does not fear, they continue contacting him. At the same time they are studying the people..."

"They control everything with the power of the mind, which, they told me, was of extreme importance. During our conversation I asked them, 'Why did you select my husband for this problem? And they responded that any person here in the universe could be selected. Right now is a period of experimentation, but later, there will be millions who will see them, (1995. UFOs sighting in Mexico) they do not want to endanger humanity. They come here to help us. We are extremely backward, in everything, they say."

Then Filiberto Cardenas spoke to the investigators. "I cannot repeat all that they told me aboard the ship, but they reaffirmed that they came to planet Earth to aid us in all they could, and very especially in all related to health. They ratified their universal love concept. They do not come to endanger or to conquer us, nor do they want to be recognized as saints or saviors. This has happened before. They say that they are beings of other dimensions, of other worlds, but that they are not gods, and they do not want to be considered such. They do not want to be attacked. They want me to be one who talks to the public about these messages designed to prepare for the coming of them on Earth. These messages have been given to six other people of Earth who have been contacted of this kind or will be contacted soon. I do not know for sure whether these other six are abductees or whether they are being contacted mentally to receive the messages. I have the impression that some are abductees, having the opportunity to see and feel directly the same as I."

"Among the things that I was told was an assurance that women will rise to important positions in our society. It is to be that many women throughout this Earth will rise to high positions in politics as well as in business. There will be a tendency to defer to and to vote for women in those positions with the hope of a change, and to see if the world can grow up. This tendency, the entities see in the very near future."

"When they come to make definite contact with us, illness will be a thing of the past. The sick will be cured easily. Anxiety is part of our evolution. This is one of the worst illnesses. Excessive preoccupation with material things, with lack of spirituality, produces the majority of illness..."

"They told me that, in the near future, we will undergo radical changes...They possess great destructive power through their scientific advancement, but they told me that they have no desire to destroy us. They live looking for and giving love..."

What make rare of this case, in the ufology history, is the second encounter, where a second person, Iris, went voluntarily to the encounter. Also, it is rare that we receive news of the sighting of UFOs at the same time and place, from independent witnesses. These make the Filiberto and Iris second encounter credible.

On December 6, 1985, Filiberto claimed that he was abducted again and carried to the same base under sea. For that motive, on March 30, 1986 we did another hypnotic regression. This time we had a different team, headed by psychologist and hypnotist Mercy de Armas, also present was hypnotist Rodolfo Morales. We took this opportunity to scan, back and forward, the first abducction. And the result was astonishing. It was like renting the same video movie, six years later, and playing it back and forward trying to find a gap. Filiberto's encounters in 1985 produce some more messages. Close to the end of this session, we made Filiberto revive the moment in which the entities put him a helmet full of needles. At that moment, Filiberto, opened his eyes full of terror, and screaming, he jump from the divan he was laying on, knocking Mrs. De Armas off her seat. I let my papers to fall to the floor and embraced Filiberto, asking him to calm down and to wake up. Another astonishing experience with Filiberto occurs in 1979, during a hypnotic session done by hypnotist Jose Yedra. It was the first time Yedra was dealing with an abduction case, and he wasn't sure of Filiberto. At one moment in the session, he pulled out of his pocket a needle and pinched Filiberto several times in the arm. Not a single muscle on Filiberto face moved. Yedra later confessed that he did it because he had doubts that Filiberto could be faking the hypnosis.

THE MESSAGES
(Taken from the hypnotic regressions)

"Look, 10,000 years before your time, this other place was created here where people live. (Referring to the place where he was taken) We are 60 times your size, and we are more powerful than you because we are more evolve than you..... There has been some 4,000 years since they began to have contact. When they gave us messages the people misinterpreted them badly. That every

100

time they have come to a particular place, they said, the people adore them as if they were gods. And they are beings superior to us but they are still far from the gods that we speak of. Some of them are well advanced, others are not. They have technical science, but they are not saints though people adore them as saints. They are preparing now, the things that are necessary so that we do not give them the reception we did in other times. It has been thousands of years since they descended last. The people then adored them and said that they were saints come to Earth."

"They told me that the distinct forms of religions, which we use, for a great part is dominated by people who seek glorification, that develop into personality cults and gain power and abundance of many things." "They told me that the leadership of the Catholic Church will be without its head (the Pope) and that later another will come." "The Pope dies, and then shortly after that the second Pope also dies. There is a struggle to designate one who is not a Roman and they told me that it would endure for a little time, but that there is a conspiracy against him. After that will come one who is not born in that place (Italy). He is going to discover the New World. He is going to come to preach to the New World in our own language." (And so it happened.)"They showed me important things. Things that they can make appear and disappear in front of one's eyes. Not only can their ships do this......" They could make us disappear into pieces in 20 minutes, or in the same 20 minutes leave us with no armaments capable of destroying anything because they can be visible or invisible as they choose." "What they are doing with me is not a pastime, but something that is playing with the happiness and the joy, the peace and the lives of millions of beings."

Here is what they showed to Filiberto, on a thing that looked like a television set in the wall of their ship: "There is a city that is going to be destroyed. The city is called... the capital of Mexico!" (At the end of 1985, happened the disastrous earthquake that destroyed part of Mexico City)

"All, almost all the great population centers of California all will go into the sea." (Parts of the coastal lands of California, from Eureka to its border with Mexico, were swallowed by the sea, according to the magazine Newsweek of March 28, 1983, pages 22 and 23) "Here in the United States we will have an illness." (AIDS)

"There is an artist who is very famous. In politics her husband could become the president of the United States." (Here, we also have to clarify that this prediction was made before the movie star Ronald Reagan took the Presidency of the United States, and his wife, also a well known artist, was the First Lady Nancy Reagan).

"The first people they showed me (on their television) were wearing loose fitting short pants. They used something like a small cap on the head. I got the impression that they were people from another planet. But later, continuing to watch as if in a movie, I could see that these were Chinese communists. Then they must have contact with the people of Communist China. They are carrying out great experiments there. They told me that Communist China would surprise the world shortly. Soon the world will be shaken by the news that is going to come out of there." "They control them. The thing is that the world will be surprised soon at what the Chinese are going to do. It is good. It is not bad." "They have control of the Chinese. There are going to be certain changes, certain things, provoked by the Chinese because there are some negative people, or would be, and in the changes those people disappear." "They showed me an example of one who was afoot and they said, 'This was their inclination,' then the person reversed his position front to back and they said, ' This is the way China will go.' "There is a plaza with an obelisk. Beneath this obelisk there is a tomb, and beneath the tomb is another room, and under that room is the control that can paralyze cities and towns completely." "They gave those (Chinese) the control, but it is as if they have power over their minds." That moment, I asked Filiberto: Do they control the governments? "They can do this. Those who have control are not precisely in higher government. They have power,

including killing anyone who gets in their way."
"They need to expand to other places and they
want to make certain scientific tests."

As you can see, this "grays" the entities that not
only could control governments, but also could
physically eliminate whoever disturbed their
plans.

On May 4, 1989, some 100,000 pro-democracy
student activists staged a huge protest march in
Tiananmen Square in Beijing, China's capital city.
The demonstrators erected a 33-foot obelisk
entitled "Goddess of Democracy," modeled after
the Statue of Liberty in New York. Then armored
troops stormed the Square, killing an estimated
3,000-5,000, injuring another 10,000. In the ensuing
political crackdown, Zhao Ziyang was stripped of
his party post, and Jiang Zemin became general
secretary. The Eight National People's Congress
elected Jiang president of China in March 1993.

"I know what you are trying to do with me, and
they know also, and so they are telling me to
watch what I am saying. But nevertheless, though
I cannot tell you directly, it is possible for you to
guess the person. I am going to mention two. One
is the ruler of Egypt. The government of Egypt in
a short time will lose its leader. It will lose its
government and there will be great disasters
throughout its territories. It could put this whole
planet in peril of being disintegrated by a war of

great consequences. This could occur before the end of 1981." On October 6, 1981, the president of Egypt, Anwar al-Sadat, was assassinated by religious fanatics within his own army, during a military parade commemorating the Yom Kippur War.

"They want to avoid all this. In this year there is a great conspiracy against the government of Israel. At the same time there is a great conspiracy between the people that control energy, in Kuwait and also in Arabia where they have petroleum energy. All those governments will disappear."

This last message was incredibly exact. Kuwait was lost during a military struggle to Iraq, led by President Saddam Hussein, in August 1990. Under the command of U.S. General H. Norman Schwarzkopf, the multinational coalition of the United States, Saudi Arabia, Great Britain, Egypt, Syria, and France began intensive aerial bombardment of military targets in Iraq and Kuwait. In mid-February, Iraq signaled its willingness to withdraw from Kuwait. A permanent ceasefire was accepted by the allies on April 6, 1991. In 2003 a coalition led by the U.S. and U.K. invade Iraq to depose him. He was convicted of charges and was sentenced to death. He was executed in 2006.

Egypt. Hosni Mubarak stepped down after 18 days of demonstration during the 2011 Egyptian revolution after 30 years of dictatorship.

Libya. Muammar Gaddafi ruled Libya for 42 years, from 1969 to 2011. He was captured and killed by the National Transitional Council.

Syria. Basha al-Assad succeeded his father in 2000, who had ruled Syria for 30 years. At present, there is a civil war and nobody knows its end.

Libro. en Inglés, publicado en 1982

We have to remember that all these messages were given to Filiberto Cardenas during his abduction on January 3, 1979. And they were privately published by Wendelle C. Stevens, before the events happened, in "UFO CONTACT FROM UNDERSEA" by Sanchez-Stevens, in 1982.

COINCIDENTAL CASES

The experience of Filiberto Cardenas did not end with his return to our familiar world there along the Tamiami Trail. On the contrary, it only began for the rest of us and for those has been following these developments with interest.

The subject, Ufology, comprises a great scientific base for the study of this phenomenon. Evidence exists in many of the abduction cases. The witness is identified and followed for a time, then isolated and taken aboard a craft, often examined physically and sometimes by other methods, and then returned. Sometimes there are landing marks on the ground, artifacts of different kinds and sometimes a residue of some kind. There is often evidence of physical examination on the body of the abductee. Occasionally there are other witnesses to the abduction or to follow-on events.

Other cases of abduction can be compared to that of Filiberto. For example: The disappearance of Travis Walton on November 5, 1975, when he also was taken aboard a UFO in full view of other witnesses. There, several beings of different aspect place a mask of some kind over his face. In Brazil in the Bebedouro case, witness Jose Antonio Da Silva was introduced through a door into a cubical compartment. He felt pushed and obliged to sit on a seat and they placed over his head a helmet like the one they wore. In Argentina, in the Urruti case of 1976 he says, "After the luminous flash it seemed like I was swallowed by a sort of (huge) oyster that went into a tunnel of intense violet or yellow color. I felt them (the beings aboard) put a helmet on my head that had various cables coming out of it. I felt it pressing on my parietals and the maxillaries." As in the Cardenas case, these entities transported Urruti to a submarine base where also there were humans. During the UFO wave of 1973, in October, Charles Hixon and Calvin Parker were abducted by strange beings from a UFO. Here also there are coincidences. During my interview with Hixon he said: "They were only five feet tall...my feet never touched the floor...I was moved like floating...Calvin and I have talked about this and we have come to the conclusion that they could have been robots or machines. We felt that they were programming us. They came here to do something specific, and they did it. They were not distracted by anything. I will believe, until the day I die, that they were robots communicating with a mind someplace else." Herbert Schirmer, a policeman patrolling the roads of Ashland, Nebraska, was abducted and carried someplace aboard a UFO on December 3, 1967. Reporting his abduction and what it took place he said: "There were pictures like television...On the left side of the breast they wore an emblem of a serpent...(And the sketch of that emblem was almost the same as the sketch Iris had made of the emblem they had seen in this case.) Their uniform ended on their heads in the form of a helmet with an antenna from an earphone on the left side. They told me that they have bases under the ocean near the coast of Florida, also at the North Pole, South Pole and off the coast of Argentina, all below the sea. They used the word 'invasion' in a friendly manner. They said that in one day they would show themselves completely. The public has nothing to fear from them. We should give serious consideration to the fact that they are not hostile. We have nothing to fear." The abduction of Betty Andreason Lucas occurred on January 25, 1967, one of the biggest years for UFO activity, and was investigated ten years later by Raymond Fowler, at that time, a Regional Director of MUFON in Seguin, Texas. This case was not published until six months after the abduction of Mr. Cardenas. Mrs. Andreason was abducted by small creatures who took her to an undersea base. Here also, there are similarities with the Cardenas case. During the hypnosis session Mrs. Andreason said: "Oh, and there's some water. We're going to crash into some water. Ohhh!...Oh, there is water coming up! That whole window is water, like in water! It's just a big, big, looks like a big cave or tunnel of ice with icicles all over, but there's light around it".   "They (the entities) love the human race. They have come to help us...Love is the great force...They want no harm to come to anybody...They said they had contacted others here...Others have their minds programmed...They put a secret in my mind...It will be revealed when time arrives... (It seems that many of the abductees have been programmed for the future.) I saw a pyramid...one of whose side was white..." (Here also, we have a pyramid described.)

In June of 1979, five months after the abduction of Filiberto Cardenas, in a construction near the town of Mirassol, in Brazil, Antonio Ferreira, the guard of the place, was abducted by entities. Two hours later, he was returned to the same place exhibiting the same marks on his body as Cardenas and he gave the same descriptions of events under hypnotic regression. This case was followed to see if Ferreira was in fact one of the other six mentioned to Cardenas, and it looks it was.

Other details often encountered in abduction cases are the lights and sound at the moment of the abduction. These factors of light and sound are reported in the majority of abduction cases, and very frequently in sighting cases as well. The complete loss of power in automobiles and electrical systems is also frequently reported in UFO cases of all kinds. In other UFO cases there has been observed loss of line voltage in electromagnetic systems up to and even including complete line failure for systems up to total blackout of whole large cities.

The physical characteristics of these entities are fairly common. There are differences in some aspects and in size but in general they are very similar to humans, having a head with 3-D vision, stereo hearing and other senses, a body, two arms and two legs, and they are invariably biped and walk erect. The suit or uniforms worn by these entities are surprisingly similar in general terms. They are usually a one piece close fitting garments of simple design with no evidence of closures such as buttons, zippers, etc., and occasionally have provisions for environmental systems for the occupant. The physical effect of floating instead of walking is another factor that comes up often, as does the loss of a sense of motion and time. Also it seems that inside the ship, the witness loss his sense of weight, and seldom sit to rest. Another common aspect is that these entities themselves float a little bit above the floor instead of walking. The configuration of the ship is often rounded, in the form of a plate, circular, etc., looks metallic, often has lights and sometimes sound which is frequently described as an electrical hum, or like a "swarm of bees". A physical examination of the abducted human also seems to be a frequent occurrence in this kind of case. Often this treatment leaves marks on the body. Sometimes the entities take special interest in the reproductive organs of the human being such as in the Cardenas's case. Others have been submitted to tests of various kinds. In the case of women, there are recurring reports of the insertion of a needle in the abdomen resulting in some pain. There are cases, as in that of Antonio Villas Boas, where the captive human is obliged to have carnal contact with a woman entity, evidently in connection with some genetic experiment of theirs. Cardenas's abductors told him that they had conducted similar experiments ultimately resulting in 81 hybrids, half entity, half human beings alive and well on our Earth today.

The list of such cases and the data is interminable and it is not our intent to explore it all. We offer this data to be numbered as a simple reference for the student and lecture. We do not seek to impose our ideas and deductions on anyone and leave the proper judgment of the Filiberto Cardenas case to the future.

PERSONAL POINTS OF VIEW

I cannot terminate this report without exploring several points of general interest in the Cardenas case as well as in the entire UFO phenomenon. I have tried to be as objective as possible, maintaining a scientific approach and basing our actions exclusively on the information obtained during the investigation, which often was cold and monotonous. But this was our task, to present the evidence as we studied it. But we could not let pass our reactions end emotions. Without doubt, it was a great adventure for us and the emotions were most varied, sometimes confused and other times doubtful. I believe that from the first inkling that I was confronted with a serious contact, I decided to try to involve myself in it. I tried to experience together with Mr. Cardenas, the consequences of his encounter and I must confess that this was not difficult. The psychological impact of the phenomena could be transferred to those concerned. The physical aspect of such contact could be studied extensively such as flight patterns, velocity, marks left on the ground and also on a witness's body, photographs, radar returns, etc., but the psychic or paranormal aspect has always been a difficult situation to understand, not only because we lack instruments to study it, but also because it still is not acceptable to orthodox science. Not only do we not give it scientific validity, we call it scientific irresponsibility. Nevertheless, the number of events continues to grow and they become more and more spectacular. New aspects develop which cannot be divorced from the rest of the phenomena as such. Among these are, new and different information coming from the abductees, materializations and dematerializations, not only of UFOs but of the apparent humanoids operating them as well. There have been changes of form, instant accelerations and sudden changes of position that could only be explained by aberrations in time, many of these reports are well supported by documentation of other evidence besides the witnesses which we can lay aside or ignore as we choose. Some of this includes the paranormal or psychic aspects of the UFO phenomenon.

In the Cardenas case, we find no lack of paranormal or physic aspect. If we think we have discovered a key to the phenomenon, we must study, nay, we have the obligation to study that well. We must involve ourselves in the phenomena and even try to become a part of it, feeling in our own being the effects of the phenomena. Only in this manner can we even begin to explain the events and try to encounter the truths here. It was with this foundation of belief that I entered the Cardenas case, trying to become a part of it, trying to participate together with Cardenas in what was unfolding here. We have spent almost six month with him, literally day and night during this investigation. We were in contact with him at least weekly and sometimes daily throughout this time, depending on the situation or some particular avenue of pursuit. Little by little we became accustomed to the surprises until the initial symptoms of shock disappeared. Today, more than 34 years after the Cardenas experiences, the paranormal or psychic phenomena has ceased and been replace by the normality's prevailing before the abduction. Even my wife and Mario Rodriguez have returned to normal life since the cessation of the paranormal interference. In connection with this I must report that the sounds and telepathic transmissions that they were receiving in their ears have diminished in time until today they are very infrequent or nonexistent altogether, also the strange synchronization of the three of us has failed.

We were unable, with all this information in our hands, to come to specific conclusions concerning this phenomenon which none of us really understands. At this point I think that in cases of this kind, the investigator should, and has the right, to involve him directly in the case itself if this is possible though I think that this could affect his ability to remain truly scientific. There are always others who could step in and keep the case on a scientific and objective keel if necessary.

I must confess that at the beginning of this case, when I began involving myself in the developing events, I was somewhat confused and confounded. Sometimes I did not understand which was reality and which was phenomenon, what were fact and what coincidence was. There were times when I was afraid, especially for my wife Maria Elena, afraid of what might happen still. At times I throughout that we, or she, might also have an encounter and worried a great deal about the insecurity of return. True, they returned Mr. Cardenas, but in the hypnotic regressions we learned that there are others that had not been returned.

Many times I throughout that if I involved myself much in this case, I would have to seek help from other investigators, from another with some experience in this subject, who could continue the investigation from outside the phenomena that were going on. I did not welcome this sensation and believed that it could take a will of iron to become involved to any extent without beginning to fantasize. Still becoming involved in the case itself, one could also "taste" the phenomenon. In my case I believe I lived the phenomenon without any aftereffect. Because of this it is my opinion that an investigator should become a part of the case going on, especially since there are seemingly no two cases the same. To the paranormal aspect of this phenomena different people react in different ways. They understand what they perceive from different points of view and relate it positively or negatively according to their inclination. The cultural and religious status of contactees and abductees enormously influences their interpretations and descriptions of their perceptions experienced.

We are extending the physical phenomena of the UFO question into the metaphysical. We must use our imagination therefore to carefully guide the course of the investigation, neither disillusioning ourselves nor ignoring the evidence. As well as the physical aspect, the psychic aspect demonstrates the plurality of the phenomenon at hand and its impact on the life of mankind. We must be careful, however, of the importance we place on the predictions of futures events even though they come true as outlined. There is a danger of this evolving into a religious fervor and false hope that the extraterrestrial are some kind of super beings who are here to save humanity. We must take into account the popular interest in the whole phenomenon. More than 85% of our population now believes that there is something to the UFO question and many of these think that we are in fact being visited by beings from another world. More than fifty millions of North Americans have reported seeing UFOs or knowing someone else who has seen one. We have even observed the creation of sects admiring the UFO and their occupants, and some are preparing actively for the arrival of these extraterrestrial beings. In some cases the occupants of the UFOs have told their Earth contacts that all of the problems that vex our society are our own creations and that nobody is coming from anywhere to save us from ourselves. This has been going on for more than 60 years now in its modern interpretation and it continues today in ever increasing intensity. The messages delivered and the predictions made are very similar but they are soon forgotten in the excitement of the next major case to come along. They leave their mark in time, marks that may be leading up to something of which we are at present completely ignorant. Dr. J. Allen Hynek said, "There are no experts on these things and that until we dredge up the hard data or the wreckage or get the door of the damn thing, we are just simply groping in the dark". Perhaps one day we will get to the bottom of this phenomenon. Until them, we must continue our investigations and documentation of data for study and file. Time will provide us the key to this mystery.

Chapter Four

Puerto Rico

Case: Lydda Noriega

In 1986, we had the opportunity to communicate, during her hypnosis, with the "alien entity" that manipulated the abductees. In the conversation, we touch different topics.

The Abduction

The abduction occurred on July 6, 1979 in Puerto Rico. Ms. Lydda Noriega was driving her car on Highway Guaynabo. It was 5.15 pm and the sky was sunny clear. Suddenly everything was dark; Lydda thought it was going to rain. "It looked as it was covered with a blanket, everything was very dark. I was very nervous. I began to mourn and cry," she said during hypnosis. At that time, she could see that there was an "entity" sitting beside her in the car. The next thing she remembers is that she was sitting in a room with four other "entities". Lydda was kidnapped for five days, after which she was returned to her car but in another city. Following her abduction, her marriage ended in divorce, and her friends turned their backs. Lydda, a native of Colombia, had won several beauty contests. Her husband, a prominent businessman in Puerto Rico, did not believe in her disappearance. Eventually they divorced; she lost everything and moved to Miami, dedicated to sewing. Wanting to know what happened in those five days, Lydda made contact with us. We did two regressions, the first on March 17 and the second on May 25 of 1986. During the hypnosis, we took her back from March 17 to June 6, 1979, at 5.00 pm. A few excerpts from the hypnotic regressions:

VSO- "What is happening?"
Lydda- "There is a lot of sun...but not now...I think it is going to rain...everything is very dark...I am getting very nervous...There is a blanket on top of me."
VSO- "Are you alone?"
Lydda- "With my friends...there are many...they are smaller than me...very beautiful...they are not like me."
VSO- "Describe them to me."
Lydda- "Some of them are wearing strange hats and others have nothing...they don't have hair...small but beautiful eyes...the clothes are like the ones they use to go to the moon, white..."
VSO- "How many are there?"
Lydda- "There are nine...four are women."
VSO- "How do you know they are women?"
Lydda- "Because they have small bosoms."
VSO- "What are they saying?"
Lydda- "They are saying that they are different and that you will never understand, because here,

they are all different...they all have strange names."

VSO- "Where are you?"

Lydda- "I am sitting next to my friend EKNOCK...he is lovely and affectionate."

VSO- "Can you ask him why you are with them?"

Lydda- "Because they have been monitoring me, all my life."

VSO- "Have they contacted you before?"

Lydda- "Yes."

VSO- "Since your childhood?"

Lydda- "Yes."

VSO- "How old were you?"

Lydda- "They have been always with me."

VSO- "And now, why are you with them?"

Lydda- "Because I need their help?"

VSO- "What kind of help?"

Lydda- "They give me information."

VSO- "Can you tell me what kind of information?"

Lydda- "Yes."

VSO- "Tell me,"

Lydda- "Persons will come and they will give me information regarding the mission that I have."

VSO- "What is your mission?"

Lydda- "I must transmit the information."

VSO- "What type of information?"

Lydda- "To awake the people, they say we are very distracted."

VSO- "Why do they want to awake us?"

Lydda- "So that it will not be so difficult when they come."

VSO- "Did they say, when they are coming?"

Lydda- "Yes."

VSO- "When?"

Lydda- "When the destruction will start on the planet."

VSO- "They are going to show themselves to everybody?"

Lydda- "Yes."

VSO- "Physically?"

Lydda- "Yes."

VSO- "What are they going to do?"

Lydda- "They are already doing it. They started long ago."

VSO- "And what will they do?"

Lydda- "Help us."

VSO- "How long have you been with them?"

Lydda- "The time is different here..I have been here eleven years..."

VSO- "Again, why is you with them?"

Lydda- "They do not understand why a process was delayed, they were experimenting with me."

VSO- "What process?"

Lydda- "They were monitoring the process since my childhood."

VSO- "What has caused the change?"

Lydda- "I don't know they are studying me."

VSO- "Have they done anything to you?"

Lydda- "All kinds of physical tests." VSO- "Explain one."

Lydda- "Cables, they have put all sorts of cables in my body."

VSO- "Why?"

Lydda- "I do not know."

VSO- "What else have they done?"

Lydda- "Here it is different...Lab test of blood...every kind...It is not liking there (Earth)...but; there are Love. Fine...they are beautiful."

VSO- "You feel secure with them?"

Lydda- "Yes."

VSO- "Do you mind what they are doing to you?"

Lydda- "No, here everything is beautiful...I do not want to go back (Earth)...They are my friends."

VSO- "Have they said anything about us?"

Lydda- "Yes, many things that are going to happen...Wars...Antichrist...Many problems...Untruthful prophets...Nobody will love each other...They are going to help us but, it is going to take many years...People are not ready...They are preparing people in different bases."

VSO- "They have bases, here?"

Lydda- "Yes."

VSO- "Where?"

Lydda- "In different places."

VSO- "Are you on our planet?"

Lydda- "No."

VSO- "Are there humans with you?"

Lydda- "Yes."

VSO- "Do you know them? Have you ever seen them before?"

Lydda- "No, only here."

VSO- "Do you know their names?"

Lydda- "Here, they don't use names as we do on Earth; they call each other 'Brother'."

VSO- "How do you know that some of them are from Earth?"

Lydda- "They resemble me. They are dressed like me."

Hypnotist. - "We are going to advance in time one hour. Now tell us where you are."

VSO- "Where are you? Look around you and tell us, where are you?" Lydda- "Here, with my friends."

VSO- "What has happened in this past hour?"

Lydda- "They have been teaching me very interesting exercises."

VSO- "What kind of exercises?"

Lydda- "Telekinesis."

VSO- "How do they do it?"

Lydda- "Concentration."

VSO- "Do you know how to do it?"

Lydda- "I am going to learn."

Hypnotist. - "We are going to advance two hours in time."

VSO- "What is happening now?"

Lydda- "They are bathing me."

VSO- "With what?"

Lydda- "I don't know, they are using something in a bottle."

VSO- "Why don't you ask them, what is in the bottle?"

Lydda- "They don't answer everything I ask them."

VSO- "They don't speak to you?"

Lydda- "No, they have as a control panel, everything is taped and visual." VSO- "Do you know what they are using to bathe you with?"

Lydda- "It is a liquid...it is like a brush."

VSO- "Are you dressed?"

Lydda- "No."

VSO- "Then you are naked, I assume."

Lydda- "Yes."

VSO- "How long have you been naked?"

Lydda- "I do not know, the time is so different." She answered the last part a little bit vaguely.

VSO- "Why are they bathing you?"

Lydda- "I don't know. I think it is because of contamination...you know all the sickness we have on Earth...It is a very smooth liquid...The smell is a little strong."

VSO- "What does it smell like?"

Lydda- "It is like oil...it does not stick to the skin."

VSO- "Does it have any color?"

Lydda- "No."

VSO- "They already bathed you. What are they doing now?"

Lydda- "little calisthenics."

VSO- "What else?"

Lydda- "They are shaving my head."

VSO- "They cut your hair?"

Lydda- "Yes, my hair was long and pretty."

VSO- "Why did they cut your hair?"

Lydda- "I don't want to say." She said this firmly.

VSO- "Did they harm you? Did they touch you?"

Lydda- "No."

VSO- "Did you have any sexual encounters with any of the entities?" Lydda- "No, they are good... Lovely."

VSO- "All right, what is going on now?"

Lydda- "I am getting dressed. It is very difficult. It is so wide, tangled." VSO- "All right, you are dressed."

Lydda- "Yes."

VSO- "What else is going on?"

Lydda- "We have a reunion"

VSO- "What kind of a reunion?"

Lydda- "They are working on three persons."

VSO- "The three persons are from Earth?"

Lydda- "Yes."

VSO- "Are you one of them?"

Lydda- "Yes."

VSO- "Do you know the other two?"

Lydda- "There are three...two women and a man."

VSO- "Then there are four persons from Earth, right?"

Lydda- "Yes, three and me."

VSO- "Have you talked to them?"

Lydda- "Yes."

VSO- "Do you know their names?

Lydda- "The man, his name is Carlos."

VSO- "Did he give you a last name?"

Lydda- "No."

VSO- "What are the names of the women?"

Lydda- "One is called Cielo and the other is called Carmen."

VSO- "Do you know what part of Earth they come from?"

Lydda- "Carlos is from Peru."

VSO- "And, Cielo?"

Lydda- "Brazil."

VSO- "Carmen, where did she come from?"

Lydda- "She is from Colombia, like me."

VSO- "What language does Cielo speak?"

Lydda- "Spanish."

VSO- "They were abducted the same day you were?"

Lydda- "No, one of them has been here years before me."

VSO- "Ask Carlos his last name."

Lydda- "His last name is, Check. Carlos Check."

VSO- "Ask him, what city is he from?"

Lydda- "Cuzco."

VSO- "Ask his complete address."

Lydda- After a pause. "He does not answer me."

VSO- "Ask Cielo, what city is she from?"

Lydda- "Bello Horizonte."

VSO- "What street?"

Lydda- "She does not want to answer me."

VSO- "And Carmen, what city in Colombia does she come from?"

Lydda- "Antioquia."

VSO- "Can she tell us her address?"

Lydda- "Yes."

VSO- "Ask her."

Lydda- "Brooklyn, New York."

VSO- "Brooklyn. What street?"

Lydda- "10022"

VSO- "She had been a long time with them?"

Lydda- "Yes."

VSO- "How old is she?"

Lydda- "Like me" (between 45 and 55)

VSO- "Have they all received the same training?"

Lydda- "Yes."

VSO- "What are they trained for?"

Lydda- "Chaotic events on Earth...They are preparing us."

VSO- "Did they tell you when this is going to happen?"

Lydda- "No."

Hypnotist - "Let us advance one hour later. Where are you?"

Lydda- "Receiving information."

VSO- "How do you feel?"

Lydda- "Here you never sleep...There is no rest...you don't feel tired."

VSO- "Look around, what do you see?"

Lydda- "Pyramids. They are different."

VSO- "Why different?"

Lydda- "They are like toys, different sizes of quartz."

VSO- "Toys? They play with them?"

Lydda- "They are like medicines."

VSO- "They have sickness?"

Lydda- "We bring them."

VSO- "What other things have you seen?"

Lydda- "Symbols with colors."

VSO- "What do they look like?"

Lydda- "There is a man riding in a car...it has wheels...Only two."

VSO- "Are you seeing any other symbols?"

Lydda- "Yes."

VSO- "Describe it."

Lydda- "It is a disk with something. These are decorations on the walls." VSO- "Is there light in that place?"

Lydda- "The walls are fluorescent...there is no lamp."

VSO- "Are there any entities with you now?"

Lydda- "Yes."

VSO- "How many?"

Lydda- "Nine."

VSO- "They all look alike?"

Lydda- "Yes."

VSO- "What are they doing?"

Lydda- "They are always active, doing things all the time."

VSO- "What else have they done to you?"

Lydda- "They checked my fuses in all of my body...The heart."

VSO- "What are the fuses?"

Lydda- "My chakras." (Spiritual centers of the body).

VSO- "From where do they get that information?"

Lydda- "It looks like a computer machine."

Hypnotist.- "Let us advance an hour into time."

VSO- "Where are you?"

Lydda- "We are sitting...my friends from over there (Earth)...and the ones here."

VSO- "What are you doing?"

Lydda- "We are eating food."

VSO- "What food?"

Lydda- "I don't know how to explain it, it is not liquid or solid, and it is like a white cream."

VSO- "Does it taste good?"

Lydda- "Yes...like oats."

VSO- "Did you have something to drink?"

Lydda- "Yes, water...lots of water."

VSO- "Where did you drink water?"

Lydda- "In a glass, beautiful, pure crystal."

VSO- "What else?"

Lydda- "They say that you take too much time thinking about them instead of doing something useful...We need help."

VSO- "What else?"

Lydda- "They transmit everything with telepathic cards."

VSO- "What kinds of cards?"

Lydda- "They look like blackboards."

VSO- "Ask if I can talk to them."

Lydda- "Eknock said only with you." (There are three other persons in the room with me.)

VSO- "Ask Eknock if I can talk with him through you?"

Lydda- "He said he did not want to talk."

VSO- "Why not?"

Lydda- "Because you have your people."

VSO- "Tell him I want to talk to him."

Lydda- (Silence)

VSO- "Are you asking him?"

Lydda- "Yes."

VSO- "What did he say?"

Lydda- "He said to be persistent, and not to let you get confused. To continue with your work."

VSO- "How can I get confused?"

Lydda- "In your journey."

VSO- "Is he going to help me?"

Lydda- "Yes."

VSO- "How will I know that he is helping me?"

Lydda- "You are going to receive a telepathic communication together with your terrestrial companion. You have to form a team to help humanity. Eknock said to continue your investigation. You have to select the people of your team."

VSO- "What is their goal?"

Lydda- "That you do a good job."

VSO- "For?"

Lydda - "To help planet Earth."

VSO- "Can they help us?"

Lydda- "Yes. They have been helping us for a long time."

VSO- "Have they made contact with us before?"

Lydda- "Yes, many times."

VSO- "Since when?"

Lydda- "Since 1976."

VSO- "And before?"

Lydda- "Yes."

VSO- "When?"

Lydda- "I don't ask him."

VSO- "Ask him."

Lydda - (Silence)

VSO- "Did you ask him?"

Lydda- "Yes."

VSO- "What did he say?"

Lydda- "You know."

VSO- "I would like to hear it from him."

Lydda- "When you were 13 years old."

VSO- "What happened?"

Lydda- "He say that you know. You are very complicated. Always asking for proofs, asking questions, giving problems."

VSO- "Ask him if they are the only one with us."

Lydda- "No."

VSO- "The others, how do they look?"

Lydda- "There are good ones and bad ones."

VSO- "Have the bad ones made contact with me?"

Lydda- "No."

VSO- "Is he sure?"

Lydda- "He is sure."

VSO- "But they can make contact and distract me?"

Lydda- "He says everything is going to be all right."

VSO- "He knows the others? Does he know how they look?"

Lydda- "They are different in each dimension. But, he cannot enter in everyone."

VSO- "The bad one causes evil things on Earth?"

Lydda- "Some."

VSO- "Can they be stopped?"

Lydda- "They are stopping them."

VSO- "Is that the problem he says we have?"

Lydda- "Yes."

VSO- "Are we between two forces?"

Lydda- "Yes, they stopped the turn they were giving to the Earth's poles." VSO- "Who is causing the destruction?"

Lydda- "Human beings."

VSO- "Are we being influenced? By whom?"

Lydda- "Ignorance, total ignorance."

VSO- "Can he tell me the day?"

Lydda- "Nine years after 1986."

VSO- "In 1994?"

Lydda- "Yes."

VSO- "Where, in what part of the Earth?"

Lydda- "California."

VSO- "Natural events or wars?"

Lydda - "Earthquake."

VSO- "They are going to cause this?"

Lydda- "Nobody can stop it."

VSO- "How can we help?"

Lydda- "Preparing those people that are not ready."

VSO- "Telling them to leave California?"

Lydda- "No."

VSO- "How then?"

Lydda- "Helping them so that they won't die from panic?"

VSO- "How can I do it?"

Lydda- "They will give us the knowledge."

VSO- "Can we do anything to prevent it"

Lydda- "No, this is the law of nature."

VSO- "If it is a natural disaster, how come, they know about it? Did they will tell me how to avoid it?"

Lydda- "They are not going to tell you now. Eknock says that you are doing a good job."

VSO- "But I need to know now, I need proof."

Lydda- "You are always saying that they want to manipulate you, but you are the one trying to manipulate them."

VSO- "I would like to know how they think."

Lydda- "They say that we are all crazy."

VSO- "Oh really! So, I am crazy?"

Lydda- "Yes."

VSO- "Don't they have any crazy people in his world?"

Lydda- "Yes."

VSO- "Good. Then we are both crazy." We laughed. We felt good since we were all tense. To end our conversation, I asked him if he could give me a physical proof, like a day, month, or time. After a long silence, I told Lydda to ask him again.

Lydda- "He says that you are not ready."

VSO- "When will I be?"

Lydda- "When you will be ready."

VSO- "Will I see him then?"

Lydda- "Yes."

VSO- "Will I be abducted?"

Lydda- "No."

Hypnotizer - "We will travel in time and we will advance two hours."

This was repeated two or three times before she answered affirmatively to it.

Hypnotizer. - "What are you doing?"

Lydda- "Preparing cards."

Hypnotizer - "What are you doing with the cards, preparing them in what way?"

Lydda- "Putting them in order."

Hypnotizer - "In order? Why?"

Lydda- "I can't tell you."

Hypnotizer - "Now at the count of 3 you will be at June 7, 1979 at 12:55 A.M. ONE, TWO, And THREE." VSO- "Where are you?"

Lydda- "Traveling."

VSO- "Where are you going?"

Lydda- "I don't want to go."

She was becoming very nervous

Hypnotizer - "Now at the count of 3, you will narrate your story but you will be very calm. ONE, TWO, THREE."

VSO- "Where are you going?"

Lydda- "To that hell."

VSO- "Where?"

Lydda- "I am in one of their airplanes?"

VSO- "What do they look like?"

Lydda- "Oh, they are beautiful."

VSO- "Give me a description."

Lydda- "It has 16 windows."

VSO- "Tell me what you see through the windows."

Lydda- "Trees."

VSO- "Where are you?"

Lydda- "Now?"

VSO- "Yes."

Lydda- "We are arriving."

VSO- "Where?"

Lydda- "Earth."

VSO- "Why did they send you back?"

Lydda- "To start my work."

VSO- "Are you alone or with the other 3 humans?"

Lydda- "They left before me."

VSO- "Then, are you alone?"

Lydda- "Yes."

VSO- "Where are you now?"

Lydda- "On Earth."

VSO- "Where on Earth did they leave you?"

Lydda- "I am in my car."

VSO- "What are you doing?"

Lydda- "It is very strange."

VSO- "What is strange?"

Lydda- "Because I have a sensation like if I had been dreaming...Like if I had never left my car..."

VSO- "What time is it?"

Lydda- "One."

VSO- "Where are you?"

Lydda- "I don't know."

VSO- "Did they say goodbye to you?"

Lydda- "Yes."

VSO- "What else did they say?"

Lydda- "My job started."

VSO- "Do you remember your experience?"

Lydda- "No."

VSO- "They don't want you to remember?"

Lydda- "No."

VSO- "Why not?"

Lydda- "Because there were moments of pain and over there, there is no pain."

VSO- "Do they know, what you are saying?"

Lydda- "I don't know."

VSO- "Can you ask them?"

Lydda - (Silence)

VSO- "Did you ask them?"

Lydda- "Yes, but they are in a hurry. I want to go with them...I don't want to stay here."

She again started getting nervous and showed anxiety about going with them, so we decided to end our session.

2nd HYPNOSIS. Sunday, May 25, 1986.
This was an interesting case because of the extent of her abduction, and also, because she already had gone through 3 hypnotic regressions and they couldn't break through. So, we thought we would have the same results. It was to our surprise when we were able to break through and make the connection. We want to bring to your attention that from both hypnotic regressions, we obtained information from the entities and had a conversation with them, using Lydda as a means of communication. These are the highlights:
VSO- "Where do they say you are?"
Lydda- "In another dimension."
VSO- "Here on Earth?"
Lydda- "On another planet."
VSO- "Is Eknock with you?"
Lydda- "He is my friend. He is always with me."
VSO- "Ask him if I can talk to him."
Lydda - (Silence)
VSO- "Did you ask him?"
Lydda- "Yes."
VSO- "Ask him, where they come from."
Lydda- "He says they come from a Parallel Universe."
VSO- "Ask him, if they live in the same space."
Lydda - (Silence)
VSO- "Did you ask him?"

Lydda- "Yes. He said: No."

VSO- "Ask him if they live in the same time."

Lydda - (Silence)

VSO- "Did you ask him?"

Lydda- "He says that it is not your time. Time is not very important for them, but it is for you."

VSO- "They live with us on Earth?"

Lydda -"When they need to."

VSO- "Have they made experiments with animals?"

Lydda- (Silence)

VSO- "Ask him."

Lydda - "He says that you call them Mascots."

VSO- "How long have they been here on Earth?"

Lydda- "Always."

VSO- Has they lost any craft here on Earth?"

Lydda- They have had many problems with craft."

VSO- Ask him when was the last time they had problems."

Lydda- (Silence)

VSO- "Did you ask him?"

Lydda- "He says he does not have that information"

VSO- "Ask him what kind of force or energy do they use for their craft." Lydda- (Silence)

VSO- "Did you ask him?"

Lydda- "Yes."

VSO- "What did he say?"

Lydda- "He is not going to answer."

VSO- "He does not want to answer, or he does not know the answer?" Lydda - (Silence)

VSO- "Ask him."

Lydda- "He is not paying attention to my question."

VSO- "He is not near you?"

Lydda- "Yes."

VSO- "Is he watching you?"

Lydda- "Yes."

VSO- "Ask him, why doesn't he answer?"

Lydda- (Silence)

VSO- "Did you ask him?"

Lydda- "He says that this is an annoyance."

VSO- "Ask him if they are more advanced than us."

Lydda- (Silence)

VSO- "Did you ask him?"

Lydda- "I think he is getting annoyed."

VSO- "Tell him that I don't want to bother him, and make him angry. I just want to know how much time it will take us to be like them."

Lydda- (Silence)

VSO- "Did you ask him?"

Lydda- "He says that the time here runs very fast. It is very different from where they come from; over there the time is precious, like the vital energy. You waste your time."

VSO- "Ask him what is the vital energy."

Lydda- "He says that you are making it all very difficult, that there will be no more communication."

VSO- "Can we live in their dimension?"

Lydda- "Of course."

VSO- "What must one do to enter that dimension?"

Lydda- "Wait for them. To be prepared and to prepare others."

VSO- "Would other worlds exist like ours? Do other worlds have a person that looks like us?"

Lydda- "Yes."

VSO- "Are we going to know other worlds like yours?"

Lydda- "Only the chosen ones."

VSO- "Do you have a God?"

Lydda- "God?"

VSO- "Yes, a Creator."

Lydda- "Yes."

VSO- "The same God we have?"

Lydda- "The same."

VSO- "Are you immortal?"

Lydda- "Yes."

VSO- "You have always existed?"

Lydda- "Always."

VSO- "You will always exist?"

Lydda- "Forever."

VSO- "You always live calmly?"

Lydda- "Yes."

VSO- "Is there other methods of communication besides this one?

Lydda- "You got involved in this...You solve it...Let's see how you do it."

End of hypnosis.

The years have gone by, and we lost track of Lydda, but recently, we heard life has not been easy for her. Was her mission accomplished? We don't know, but what we know is that her experience altered her life to the point that she lost all hope of happiness, and at this point, she has nothing. Because of her experience, she feels lost in this world. Some people believe in these experiences, others not. Will you? Of course, there are always the disbelievers; the world is full of them.

Chapter Five

Florida

Deborah's Experiences.

In 1989, we were invited to give a talk, in Tampa, Florida, for the local MUFON organization. We presented the abduction of Filiberto Cardenas. When we finished, we were approached by several concurrent with your questions, including a lady who said she had experienced a missing time, when she was 12 years old, in the backyard while playing with her friend Linda. She was very interested in knowing what happened and wanted a hypnotic regression to know what had happened in that missing time. We made an appointment to interview her the following week in Miami.

During the interview, we asked for details she could remember, before and after her missing time. In addition, she asked us to clarify the sighting of a ray of light she saw in the summer of 1977, and also, when she was with her husband on a vacation, a ghost that appeared in an old Victorian mansion turned hotel, where they spent a night.

For the technical part, we employed a professional hypnotist (I reserve the name). We rented a VHS video camera and bought a professional VHS cassette. We recorded the whole regression. The hypnotist asked me to borrow the video to see it. Since we personally knew him from some time ago, I did. A few weeks later we visited and asked him to return the video; he gave me an excuse, and we returned home without it. It took months, years, and he always gave me some excuse for not giving it back, although we kept a good friendship. My wife Maria Elena asked me, every time we visited him, not to insist. I gave it up for lost.

Two years, after Willy Smith's death in 2006, his widow called me and asked me if I wanted some videos of Willy's, because if I wear not interested, she was going to throw them in the garbage. I picked up about 15 videos and started, from time to time, to watch them. Three years passed and, in 2011, in one of them appeared Deborah's regression, mixed up with other programs. It was a surprise! I did not remember Willy making a copy; and, coincidentally, it happened to be at a time when I started to prepare this book. After 22, years, I was able to locate Deborah, visit her, and give her a copy of the video. In our meeting, Deborah confessed that, because of her UFO experiences with extraterrestrials, she had developed psychic ability and used it to help those in needs. In those 22 years, she had traveled, giving lectures and interviews on television, about how, combining brain power with medicine, could alleviate many diseases. She is well known and has written books on the subject. She gave me permission to write about her experiences, but preferred that I keep her real name anonymous. She said her regressions were very personal.

Following is a summary of the questions asked during regression:

Virgilio Sanchez-Ocejo. - You're with your friend Linda, playing in the backyard of your home. Tell me, what is happening?

Deborah. - I saw a white light. There was more than one light. I was afraid.

V S-O. - What do you see?

Deborah. - I try to see, but I see nothing. I am lying. I don't know where I am.

V S-O.- You were in the backyard fence with your friend Linda. What happened?

Deborah. - I was with them.

V S-O. - Who are they?

Deborah. – I don't know.

V S-O. - What is it?

Deborah. - I cannot see them.

V S-O. - How do you know you are with them?

Deborah. - Because I feel them.

V S-O. - Where are you?

Deborah. - I'm sitting. I'm with them. They are looking at me.

V S-O. – They kidnapped you?

Deborah. - Yes.

V S-O. - Would you describe where you are?

Deborah. - They are watching me. I see, like, faces. They are observing me.

V S-O. - Would you describe their faces?

Deborah. - They have something in their hands. Something likes silver, like a silver wand. They wrote something. I could touch the rod, and it hurt me, made me feel very bad.

V S-O. - They talked among themselves?

Deborah. - I did not understand what they said. They looked at me and talked about me, about who I am. They said that I was a human species. Now, someone entered, someone with a strong

146

power. I felt it. He was one of them. There was not a male or a female. They had no sex. They were only energies. I could see his eyes were gray, white in the middle. I don't know what they wanted with me. They had hands with five fingers. I wanted to see everything. They were very tall, and had ears, small noses, no hair, clear white skin. They were dressed in white coats like doctors. The walls were ash-colored, with a smooth ceiling. They did not communicate with me; the only thing they wanted is to know what I was. They did not hurt me. I think I was in a spaceship. I was in a small room.

V S-O. - How was the ship from the outside?

Deborah. - Like silver, round, with many windows, was lit inside. It made no noise.

V S-O. - What day is it?

Deborah. - Saturday, May 30, 1959. I was 12.

V S-O. - Where's Linda? (Her friend).

Deborah. - On the fence. She is paralyzed.

V S-O. - Why they took only you?

Deborah. - They wanted to teach me.

V S-O. - What do they want to teach you?

147

Deborah. - About them. They were here with us, on this planet with us. They mingled among them with us. They taught me to be like them. Do things. See the differences between people. They taught me love, how to love, be good. Knowing things like fear some people fear. View inside or inside things to my knowledge. They chose me because they liked me. I spent an hour with them and then they returned me with a white beam of light to the fence (in the backyard). My girlfriend was sitting paralyzed.

So much for the regression to the time lost. Now, follow what happened in the summer of 1977, when Deborah says she saw a flash of red light:

V S-O. - In the summer of 1977, you saw a flash of red light. Are you seeing it?

Deborah. - I see a red light. I see something in the sky. I don't know what it is. It's like a crystal. I think it's them. I am scared. I don't know what they want, I'm afraid. I was with him, with my husband Greg; he also saw the UFO. It was a UFO. This UFO was different. We saw it for 5 minutes. I wanted a closer look with binoculars, but it was the same. I did not see him leave.

V S-O. - How did you feel?

Deborah. - I felt like they pushed me through the navel.

V S-O. - You came up with this before?

Deborah. - Yes.

V S-O. – Would they put something in your belly button?

Deborah. - Yes.

V S-O. - What was it?

Deborah. - A crystal.

V S-O. - What for?

Deborah. - To communicate with me.

V S-O. – Do you still have the crystal?

Deborah. - Yes.

V S-O. - Do you still communicate with them?

Deborah. - No.

V S-O. - Why?

Deborah. - I hide.

V S-O. - Why?

Deborah. - Because I fear them.

V S-O. - Why are you afraid?

Deborah. – I could die.

V S-O. - Why do you think that?

Deborah. - Because they want to do things.

V S-O. – Like what?

Deborah. - Make sacrifices. They can hurt me.

V S-O. - Why do they say that?

Deborah. - I know.

V S-O. - Do you have that crystal in your home?

Deborah. – It's inside me. They put it inside my body.

V S-O. - Do they communicate with you very often?

Deborah. - Yes.

V S-O. - Can you avoid contact?

Deborah. - No. But sometimes they leave me alone for a while.

V S-O. - When was your first contact with them?

Deborah. – It was on the beach, when I was 4 years old.

V S-O. - What happened on the beach?

Deborah. - A wave covered me.

V S-O. - What beach?

Deborah. - In New York, during the daytime.

V S-O. - Are you alone?

Deborah. – I was with my parents, I was not alone.

V S-O. - Tell me. What happened?

Deborah. - A wave covered me, and my parents tried to find me. I was under the sea. I was lonely. I felt something pull me through my navel. My parents tried to get me out of the sea. One of them (entity) watched me while I was underwater.

V S-O. - He was underwater, too?

Deborah. - No, he was standing on the beach.

V S-O. - How did you know he was one of them?

Deborah. - I knew him; he was the one with the rod. He seemed to be made of light, like a spaceman.

V S-O. - Can you describe it to me?

Deborah. - He's bald, tall, was wearing something like a suit of several parts, silver. My parents saw him.

V SO. - Have you any other experience, before you were 4 years old?

Deborah. - I was 3 years old.

V S-O. - What happened?

Deborah. - I had a fever, was sick with fever. They visited me in my house. I was lying on the living room sofa. I was afraid. I was in the room and walked through the door. They were there.

V S-O. - Would you describe them?

Deborah. - Very tall, to the ceiling, dressed as humans. They caught me and lifted me, sheltered me. They were going to take care of me.

V SO. – Would they physically touch you in any of your experiences?

Deborah. - They marked me. They touched me amicably. They put something inside of me, but I did not feel it. I felt happy. When they touched me, they felt lukewarm, neither cold nor hot.

V S-O. - Do you feel their skin?

Deborah. - No, they gently touched.

V SO. - Do they give you any specific instructions to follow?

Deborah. - Yes. Love my fellow humans. Be good. Be alert to what happens to me.

Now we ask her about the ghost she saw in the old southern mansion converted into a hotel, where they spent one night, during a vacation trip:

V S-O. - Who is she? (In reference to the ghost)

Deborah. – She is the owner of the house. She likes this home.

V S-O. – Is she dead?

Deborah. - Just her body. She feels lonely.

V S-O. - Why does she feel lonely?

Deborah. - Because she has to be here.

V S-O. - Why?

Deborah. – She is extremely attached to her home. She cannot leave. She wants to talk to someone.

V S-O. - Can she speak to you?

Deborah. - Yes.

V S-O. - What did she say?

Deborah. - Wake up, wake up.

V S-O. – What she is wearing? Describe her?

Deborah. - She dressed in white. She has a white bow on her head. She has blue eyes. She is very pretty.

V S-O. - How did she die?

Deborah. – She fell. She died very young. She was very happy; it happened the night of her wedding.

V S-O. - What is her name?

Deborah. - Sarah Livingston.

V S-O. - What did she say?

Deborah. - She fell out the window. Someone pushed her out the window.

V S-O. - Do you know who did it?

Deborah. - Yes. Her husband pushed her.

V S-O. - Why?

Deborah. - She knows.

V S-O. – What is her husband name?

Deborah. - She is crying. He liked the roses. He died.

V S-O. – Why is she still in the house?

Deborah. - She is very sad. She cannot leave. She is shaking.

V S-O. - Did you tell her that she has to go, that she does not belong here?

Deborah. - She does not know that. She thinks she is still alive. She knows is her spirit. Her spirit is alive. I can see it. But I do not want see it.

V S-O. - Do you know when she died?

Deborah. - In 1837. She was so in love with her husband.

V S-O. – Why did he push her out the window?

Deborah. - He no longer wanted her. He is in love with another person.

V S-O. - Tell her that she has to leave, she cannot continue in that dimension.

Deborah. - I will.

V S-O. – Is there any connection with your other experiences?

Deborah. – No, none.

We end the regression with the ghost of the old mansion. Ultimately, the husband killed her, throwing her out the window of the second floor because he had an affair and wanted to inherit the property.

Recently, I traveled to the city of Tampa, where Deborah lives, and asked her, if up today she had remembered more details about her experience with Sarah's ghost? Here is her answer:

"It was an old Victorian house with trellises of roses that covered the entire front and the entrance path, which made the place unique in its class. The mansion had a turret with a window on top. The room we stayed in had old style windows with window seats. It was a very old house with one or two rooms for rent. The room had a small bed rented with or without breakfast. That night, we could find no rooms in any hotel, and we were lucky to find this place. It must have been my destiny! The ghost of Sarah Livingston held a long-stemmed rose in her ghostly hands. So it was a surprise when we went in the morning, and saw all the rose trellises covering the road. We had arrived very late the night before, and were extremely sleepy, so I didn't notice the roses. Then, the next day, before we left, we spoke with the person who rented the room to us. We were told that the rose trellises had always been there. Thus, Sarah's death must have occurred in the 1800s or at the beginning of the century. This is really a new awakening of that entire experience, and it gives me chills"

This experience occurred in Gloucester, Massachusetts. We found out, on the Internet, that there are currently seven Sarah Livingstons living in that town, who very well could be one or more of the ghost's descendants.

Yes, Sarah was a real person! Looking back on this entire experience, on, thing is for sure: either it is all true, or it is all a fantasy. We believe that all of her experiences were real. In fact, this happened to reveal a high degree of credibility regarding Deborah's experiences.

Now, we move to another experience: According to Deborah, as a child she played, with "little men". She had doubts, and wanted to ensure they were not extraterrestrials:

V S-O. - Can you tell me, who the small men are that you saw on top of your dresser?

Deborah. – Yes, they were elf creatures. I could see them when I was little. I communicated with them only once. Sometimes, I saw them dancing. They were my friends. I liked them.

V S-O. - Did they have names?

Deborah. – No, I don't know.

V S-O. – Is there a connection with your other experiences?

Deborah. - No.

V S-O. - Where did they come from?

Deborah. – They were here.

V S-O. - Did your brother see them?

Deborah. – Yes.

Finally, we asked about her relationship with her mother. According to Deborah, they fought constantly, and she wanted to know if it was created in her past life:

V S-O. - You told us, you'd had problems with your mother. In what year of life did it occur?

Deborah. - I remember it was in the '60s.

V S-O. - In this life?

Deborah. – No, a long time ago.

V S-O. - What was your relationship with her at that time?

Deborah. - She was my sister.

V S-O. - What happened?

Deborah. – We were in the field. We were discussing, fighting for a lover.

V S-O. - Who is the lover in that life?

Deborah. - Jo.. Jo.. Jo.. (Laughter) My husband!

V S-O. - Do you have a good relationship with him?

Deborah. - Yes. Very good.

V S-O. - What is your husband's name?

Deborah. - George.

V S-O. - What is the problem?

Deborah. – She, my mother, liked him, and I liked him too. I fight for him. We hauled by the hair. I beat her. That's why she hates me for what happened.

V S-O. – What was the lesson learned in this life?

Deborah. - Loving her as it is. I love her.

And here, we end with the experiences of Deborah. Comments are left to the reader.

Chapter Six

Mexico

I SLEPT IN THE TOMB OF AN ALIEN BEING!

I slept in a pyramid tomb at Palenque, and was subject to unique paranormal experiences for which, so far, I have no satisfactory explanation. I do not know it was by a force generated by the pyramid-shaped, wave reception of other beings acting upon my brain or my nervous system. What I can say, so far, is that it is a paranormal phenomenon, without sufficiently studied, and poorly understood. I reject the intervention of spiritual or religious element because such explanations are not scientifically acceptable to those, who like me, are agnostic, but admits that there may be a sense other than the familiar five senses, taught the early grades of school.

History and Mythology.

5,000 years ago, history and mythology tell us that, we were deeply backward. Suddenly, we were visited by a number of "outsiders", who taught us agriculture and the first laws, which later led us to a higher state of civilization. Some of these "strangers" are said to have come from the oceans and seas. Others are said to have descended from the heavens. They were the first "gods". The men, who had the opportunity to meet and learn from them, became kings, prophets, or priests. These men became something "divine", different from us, including their children, heir to their knowledge and powers, as the psychic ability to see and communicate with supernatural beings. Mysteries related to the creation, the origin of man, and the presence of God on Earth, have begun to be seen from new perspectives. Relentless progress in astronomy and the disturbing presence of strange objects flying through the skies, UFOs, threaten to alter traditional interpretations. One of his influences is the buildings made by our ancestors, with the knowledge acquired by extraterrestrial contact. Nowadays, these monuments still rise, defying time, cultural progress, and human technology. Fabulous palaces, temples, and buildings that were once the pride of past civilizations are today causing admiration and perplexity to those who contemplate. Still, they elicit surprise, intrigue, and confusion to those who study and try to unravel its mysteries. Among these constructions, one in particular always caught my attention perhaps, because it is the oldest of all, or perhaps because it contains so much mystery, it could fill entire libraries with all that has been written about the pyramids. Around the year 2,000 BC, three civilizations flourished in America and achieved political and cultural supremacy. These were the Inca Empire in Peru and Bolivia, the Aztecs in Mexico, and the Maya in Central America

(Guatemala, Chiapas, and Yucatan). The Mayan civilization was completely different from the other two. Today, it is only known by its ceremonial centers, palaces, public buildings, and works of art, because by the year 600 AD, and for no apparent reason, the Mayans abandoned their cities, temples, and pyramids. The jungle covered everything, and they never returned. This is unique in the history of American civilization, and perhaps in the history of the human race. What happened? Why did the Mayans leave everything, especially when they were at such a high level of civilization? Mayan mythology is unique. They claimed to have obtained the knowledge of their ancestors. Their traditions say that not only have they lived in Central America, but they came from lands across the sea. Is it possible that this refers to the lost continent of Atlantis, Mu, or Lemuria? How did they come across the sea? Mayan traditions collected many of these migrations. They came to Central America in the year 3,113 (Before Christ). That year, recently confirmed by archaeologists in excavations north of Colombia, was the chronological beginning of the Maya in America, to the arrival of the Spaniards. Mayans did not receive the Spaniards with open arms, as did the Incas and Aztecs, but rather tried to avoid contact as much as possible. Why? Because they were waiting for the "ships of Gods." How would they know they were not made of wood as Spanish vessels were? The Mayans never confused the Spaniards with the gods. Why? Why did they not recognize them as technologically superior? What kind of "craft" and gods were they expecting? Perhaps, they sought ones that were better or of another nature. Mayan writing had developed and even formed books or "codes." They refer to astronomical events that took place millions of years ago. Ancient texts tell us that the gods came to Teotihuacan and formed an assembly with the local men. This event transpired in history much earlier than "homo sapiens" were known to exist. Astrology was so important in Mayan culture that when the children reached five years old, they consulted the stars to determine their future as a soldier, peasant, or sacrifice to the gods. The Mayans were a doomed civilization. How could they know the planets Uranus and Neptune? Why were the observation posts in the observatory of Chichen-Itza not aimed at the brightest stars? What is the reason of the Mayan calendar with calculations for 400 million years? How did the Mayans know to calculate the Solar and Venusians year? Who taught them this amazing astronomical knowledge? They did not build temples and pyramids at will. Their calendar stipulates that buildings are made in parts, every 52 years. Each stone is related to their calendar, and each construction is according to astronomical requirements. The first pyramid was built in La Venta, in the southwest of Yucatan. Constructions were later spread throughout Central America. Anthropologists know that the Mayans knew the principle of the wheel. Their calendar is circular.

They did thousands of representations of the wheel, including children who had toys with wheels. Well then, why do, almost all textbooks teach us that the Mayans never "used" the wheel? Did the Mayans know the wheel, and did not bother to use it? Did they use something better for transportation than wheels? Could they have had something better than wheeled vehicles? Why did their children use it in their toys? It is well known that no one has found a Mayan road or highway, and that the cities were located well within the jungle. Therefore, we ask: If they did not use wheels or have roads and highways, how did they carried giant stones to build their temples and pyramids, if it is proven that the quarries were hundreds of miles away? Could it be that they used the same system as the Egyptians? Was there ever was contact between Mayans and Egyptians? The Mayans maintained an empire, for many centuries, without any means of communication between more than 120 cities being discovered so far. How did they live without vehicles, roads, or weapons in the jungle? Why did they build their cities in the jungle and not near a river or the sea? Certainly, one cannot answer any if he or she looks at the Mayan civilization from the traditional view. We hope that future translations of Mayan texts give us a clearer idea of their history and mythology so we can answer the 1,000 questions, without logical answers that we ask today.

PALENQUE.

 The Maya have styles of very well defined architecture, and one can easily distinguish them in their constructions of the Yucatan Peninsula. Palenque is located at the entrance of the peninsula, on the side of the earth, near the border with Guatemala, and the Sierra Madre. Many, including I, consider the archaeological site of Palenque as the most beautiful site in Mexico. One can watch the conglomerate structures half hidden in the jungle, a towering green sea of vegetation that fills me with joy and admiration. The Palenque region has the highest average rainfall in Mexico. For that reason, the structure went unnoticed, for hundreds of years; the jungle covered everything from the eyes of man. Hernan Cortes himself went about 77 kilometers away, and both he and the Indians who accompanied him were unaware of its presence. It was in 1773, that a group of Spanish friar accompanied by Ramon Ordonez y Aguiar, visited the city. Later in his book, the monk described the city as the type "Atlantis". In 1776, Captain Antonio del Rio arrived to explore Palenque. His report was lost in the archives of Madrid, and it was not until 1822 that a copy of it was published in England. This

was the first book on Palenque, which aroused the interest of archaeologists worldwide. In the year 1831, a soldier of fortune named Count Weldeck arrived in Palenque. There he remained for two years, living on top of the pyramid that now bears his name: "The Temple of the Count". He died at the age of 109 years, and his book attracted the attention of a young American explorer named John L. Stephen. Stephen visited the site in 1837, starting the first scientific study of the area. Palenque grew by 300 BC, and had its peak in the year 700 AD, the same time as that of Teotihuacan in the Valley of Mexico. Abruptly, between 1000 and 1500 AD, the city was completely abandoned, and today there is no known reason for this strange fact. The jungle covered everything. Palenque also faded from the minds of men.

Why is Palenque the goal of my desires, studies, and dreams? Given that there are not only pyramids, temples, and astronomical observatories, Palenque has been the first pyramid tomb discovered in America. However, the real reason is here. In Palenque, there was never a foreign invasion or foreign mixture with the Mayan culture. Those ruins are buildings and temples, and in their midst stands a pyramidal structure that has been preserved, which archaeologists call the "Temple of Inscriptions" because of the extraordinary amount of hieroglyphics that, so far, have not been deciphered. The pyramid consists of eight platforms and a central staircase, made of stone that has 69 steps and is 75 feet high. The inclination angle is 45 degrees. At the top of the pyramid, there is a temple. Inside the temple, there is a passage with a staircase down to the inner center of the pyramid. The staircase can reach the center and makes an angle, which begins another staircase that leads to the inner base of the pyramid, where there is a vault. At the end of it, there is a triangular, one stone door, behind which is another vault, in which there is a sarcophagus 10 feet long by 7 feet wide. The cover is made of carved smooth stone. On it are several inscriptions and bas-reliefs that depict a man in the position also adopted by current astronauts when they are inside a rocket carrying them to the moon, or orbiting the earth. This stone is 12 ½ feet long and weighs about five tons. This giant slab was built by the laborers working under the orders of Mexican archaeologist Alberto Ruz. Uncovered the sarcophagus, they found the bones of an individual. A jade mask covers the face. The individual also bears neck collars, and rings on the arms and legs, all of which are jade. In Mayan symbolism jade was the stone of the gods, as in Egypt of the Pharaohs. They took the remains to Mexico City for study in the current Museum of Anthropology of the Aztec capital. There they found that the size and characteristics of skeletal forms, given in proportion to the bones found, were different from those observed in the prototype of the Mayans. For example, the Mayans did not exceed four feet in height while the remains of this individual's sarcophagus and jade mask indicated that his or her figure reached nearly six feet in height.

After a long road trip that crosses the Sierra Madre, I was finally in this archaeological site. Now, in front of the enigmatic pyramid, I contemplated his majesty, which arose before me like an impenetrability giant. Hundreds of questions crossed my mind. It began to dawn, and the sun's rays penetrated behind the mountains around me. The dew of the night had left his garment in crystalline vegetation, giving it a wet frame of temples and pyramids, which, after being hit by sunlight, were charged with new life. For a moment, I felt I was a stranger, a defiler of sacred places, and I ask: Were these people so different and mysterious? The first construction I visited was "The Palace".

The largest and most complicated construction of Palenque. The entire building is built on an artificial platform 30 feet high. It consists of corridors, courtyards, and tunnels linking 25 quarts or bedrooms. The most mysterious and interesting part is its tower. At its highest point, carved on one of its walls, there is the astronomical symbol of Venus. In the center, there is an altar or stone table. This tower may have served as an astronomical observatory and observation tower, or as a defense of this place. Its resemblance to a Chinese pagoda made us think of a European connection. From there, we headed south of the city.

This group consists of four pyramids, three of which are named by archaeologists with Roman numerals; Temple XVIII, Temple XVIII a, and Temple XXI. The fourth is named "Temple of the Cross." This temple is the tallest of the group and has caused large discrepancies among scholars because inside, carved in stone, lies a huge cross. While we could not decipher all the hieroglyphics surrounding it, we will think that there was a connection between the god Quetzalcoatl and Jesus Christ. This made us think, too, that Mayan mythology and the mythology of the Bible are stories of true facts. Those believers of all religions, forgive me. It is not my purpose to

170

argue, or to contradict anyone. Only by speculation, through speculation, and keeping our minds open, can we understand a little more the mysteries that unfold before us. At the entrance of Temple XVIII were found three empty graves, apparently visited by looters, since no valuables were found there. Recorded on a wall, I saw the figure of a bearded man, beside which is something that might seem like a "space mask". Who was that bearded man? The Maya did not wear beards. In the temple XVIII a, we also found a grave at the end of a 10 foot tunnel.

The entrance is located in the center of the sanctuary. No one sarcophagus was found; however, the remains of an approximately 20 years old man, with a mask of jade and some jewelry, were found. Beside him, the remains of a young woman also were discovered. No one knows who these persons were because the bones were made of dust. It is speculated that subordinates to the individual were found in the Temple of the Inscriptions. There are some pieces of wall with hieroglyphs, around the tomb, but they are being deciphered. Archaeologists say that these tombs are of minor importance, that is, of lower class individuals. The main water supply of this city is the river Otulum. This river crosses from side to side the ruins. It has a small waterfall that falls into a kind of natural pool, named by archaeologists "The Queen's Bath". However, this is really the place where the priests and possibly the entity of the mysterious pyramid-tomb bathed or purified themselves. I could not control myself, and so I took off my clothes, and jumped in the cold waters. I wanted not only to see, but also feel how the local priests had felt for thousands of years.

The Mayans had a reputation for being extremely clean. They bathed more than once a day. It was customary for the man in the family, when returning from his work, to find a hot water bath, prepared by his wife. Devotion to personal cleanliness became almost fanatical. The old man always looked at cleansing or purification, as the way to get closer to God. Is it coincidence that the Mayans practiced this type of cleaning, just as today most religions require a way of purification before entering the "house of God"? Was that how the link "cleaning and likeness of God", was introduced into the mind of primitive man? All these questions ran through my mind while enjoying the crystal clear waters. However, little by little, they were becoming turbid, and we decided to leave. Later, I became aware of the presence of two crocodiles lived in the river, before the waterfall and pool where I bathed. If only I had seen them before!

To prevent flooding, because of the growing rains that hit the spot while taking advantage of the fresh water, the Mayans built an underground aqueduct. Made of reinforced stone, in some places the aqueduct reaches a depth of 6 feet. This discovery was made by collapsing part of the pipeline, exposing the construction. Even today, after thousands of years, the water still runs. In fact, you do not know its exact route, or where water starts this unique system. Other temples are in very poor condition. It was late afternoon, and it was time to carry out what I planned to do within the Temple of Inscriptions.

I started to climb the 69 steps up to the upper temple. Upon reaching the top, I turned my head and beheld a panoramic view of the place. It is amazing to watch the ruins from that point and the valley below us. The same view seeing by the chosen of that time. In the temple, I found the custodian or guardian of the place. Then, struck up a conversation with him for 30 minutes and I explained my purpose. After repeatedly saying, that there is a prohibition against what I wanted to do, he finally agrees. This temple, at the top of the pyramid, is larger than others. In the five pillars forming in front entries, are engraved in relief figures of priests. In the left column, we see a strange engraving which shows a priest in front of a woman and a child. On the back wall are three large panels carved in stone, where there are about 620 hieroglyphs. These hieroglyphics have been partially deciphered. The number 692 appears in one of them. Some scholars believe that this number represents the year of completion or dedicated the pyramid. The floor consists of large stone slabs. In one, slap were found twelve perforations or holes. This caused the archaeologist Ruz, in 1949, to suspect the existence of a secret passage. When running the slab, he found a staircase filled with stones and earth. It took two years to remove this debris, and get to the vault of the tomb.

It was about six o'clock in the afternoon, when I start down that ladder. The passage was lit by small bulbs powered by a gasoline engine generator. The standard electricity, typically supply from the town of Palenque to the ruins, had suffered a malfunction.

As I descended the stairs, the air was thinning... It seemed to be an endless tunnel. The staircase was projected downwards, so that it seemed as if I was entering a time warp... I had finally reached the end of the stairs, and I was standing in front of the vault, 12 feet long by 4 feet wide. On the walls ran a few drops of water, falling to the ground with their sounds. In the background, a triangular stone was leaning against a wall. It was the entrance to the vault with the sarcophagus.

I walked over and stood in the triangular opening. The shock was immense. Before me, it looks like it was a finished new building, as it is today, and not over 1,000 years ago, intact.

It had a large carved red slab, under which you could see the stone sarcophagus. There is little what I can say, and there are no adjectives that can express what it was exposed before me. The next few minutes I was transfixed by the stunning spectacle. I had no doubt. It was the tomb of an enigmatic and controversial person. In the relief of the red tile, you can see the figure of a Mayan, which, according to the Swiss writer Eric Von Daniken, resembles a modern spaceship. If we look at it from this point of view, its likeness looks amazing and impressive. The carving figure is dressed in the fashion of his time, sitting and locked in what could be called a jet-propelled spacecraft. His head is covered with a kind of helmet, which is in turn placed in a kind of support. There is a tube attached to the nose, oxygen provider. His hands are a kind of command, for the way in which he grips. The right foot is clearly seen as it presses a pedal. Furthermore, the left heel is put on the kind of gear wheel. There is also a belt or safety belt. All this is within a bullet-shaped cavity with its point and its metal plates riveted well defined. The engine appears to be divided into four sections and ends in a series of tubes through which flames emerge. Stabilizers and the air intake are well defined. We are facing a real and obvious fact that once would have gone unnoticed. For archaeologists, the Temple of Inscriptions is the tomb of a royal personage, very similar to the pyramids built by the Egyptians. According to archaeological books, the character found inside the sarcophagus, was a king. This king was called Pacal, and died at the age of 80 years.

Archaeologists believe that the engraving of the slab is not a technological illustration but a religious one. Looking at it, from this new point of view, it represents the transition slab of King Pacal, placing it at the time of his death, suspended between two worlds. What they do not tell us, is that the shape or symbol of the cross, is perfectly engraved on the slab. There isvery little to tell us the origin of this enigmatic King Pacal, whose height and build, recorded in various slabs, do not resemble any Mayan prototype. Are we really at the tomb of a "higher" that dates back to several centuries? Are we answering with affirmation? Wouldn't we put in doubt scientific books, in which exact science teaches its dogmas? Perhaps it is better, to remain silent...

I started taking pictures with my camera, for future studies, but electric batteries became weaker, and soon, the light bulb on magnesium or "flash" just stopped working, to my surprise, in a period of time shorter than usual. Because of this, I could not take all the pictures I had planned. It is nearing the time to do some thinking transmissions, timed with my wife, and a friend, Raul Najera, in different parts of the city of Miami, more than 2,000 miles away. I decided to sit and lie on the triangular stone at the entrance of the tomb.

Pulled out of his pocket five decks marked with different symbols: a circle, two parallel lines, a star, a cross, and a triangle. I had long been practicing translation at my home with my wife, and often, like her, managed to guess three or four letters. My clock showed 7 pm, Miami time, when I began to focus on each letter. After several minutes, I started sending a sequence of them. After a while, I focused again, and tried to guess the sequence of my wife. I put the cards that struck me in order. I waited until the clock struck 7.30 pm. This time I opened my pen, and wrote on a blank card: "The Palenque astronaut is real." This message should be the same one my friend Raul Najera wrote in Miami. I kept it all in my pocket for a future check. I had not finished saving cards, when suddenly, and to my complete surprise the lights went out, I was in complete darkness. At first I was afraid, I felt indescribable fear. I felt an intense cold in my bones. My first impulse was to get out of there, to run up the inside stairs, to the top of the pyramid and then down the outside ladder to the ground. I wanted to get away from there as soon as possible. For a moment, I hesitated, wondering whether I should or not. I thought that my journey would be in vain and that all my efforts, my studies, and

my time, depended on this moment. Little by little, I was comforted to be able to master the situation. Then, I thought of the custodian, the only one that knew I was inside the tomb. I suspected that he could enter the temple, together with someone else, and try to rob me. Before leaving Miami, my friend Raul, who is Mexican, had warned me: "Be careful, these people of the jungle do anything for a dollar." His words reverberated in my mind. I wish he had not said anything. For a moment, I thought I heard footsteps down the stairs. I was reassured, and gradually I convinced myself that there was no reason to fear. Time was passing, and slowly I began to relax. All my worries were disappearing, and I became more accustomed to the darkness, where I could not see my hands. Only the illumination of my watch dial was visible. In that moment, I realized that the footsteps I had heard were just the sound of falling water drops hitting the floor. At the end, I felt a sense of tranquility, a state of peace, or, rather, of absolute stillness. The tension was gone... I left feeling like I was in a huge room, and not in a small stone room, with its walls a few feet away... Then, the greatness of the Mayan Empire, its construction, the mysterious hidden hieroglyphics, and the image of a man whose remains had been closely guarded in the coffin that was within walking distance of me came into my mind... I could see this civilization in their daily lives. He had a mighty, short, and wide head. His hair was straight and very black. His almond-shaped eyes were dark. Besides the deformed skull, the Mayans induced strabismus. Since children, they had a basin placed between the eyes. Adult's had drawings made on their faces, through scars. They filed their teeth, and all this, was what they believed was the perfect beauty. The peasants dressed poorly, unlike the priests and the powerful, whose dress was very sumptuous. They were decorated with masks, flowers, inlaid feathers, and carved stones, and wore huge earrings, bracelets, and rings... His hair was separated by using large jade tubes, the stone preferred in all his outfits. They covered their feet with sandals adorned with different motifs. Their base food was maize. It was so important that it inspired the artists, and they came to believe that maize was his own flesh. I could see the priests, of the engravings, unique wheel connoisseur's calendar. This was a Mayan combination of mathematical and astronomical knowledge. They used to mark certain past or future events. There is an inscription of a calculation of "90 million years". I surveyed their mathematical work with a vigesimal system that included the concept of zero, a remarkable achievement in the intellectual field. I observe their hieroglyphics carved in stone, and modeled in stucco or painted in murals, ceramics, codices, and jewelry. All Mayan codices were burned by the Spanish friars. Miraculously, three were saved, namely: the Codex Disdain, with paintings of gods, the Cartesian Codex, and the Persian Codex. Thanks to the codices, we know something about Mayan astronomy, and its prediction of eclipses, ceremonies, diseases, and births. One of the unknowns of the Mayan civilization is what kind of authority ruled during the thousands of years of its existence. I could see that religion was of importance, and it is undeniable that there was a great uniformity throughout the region. The priests of various centers cooperated closely on religious matters. They extended this control, at a given time, to influence political affairs. A priestly authority may have been sufficient to maintain order. Moreover, the environment prevented the development of technical progress and high-level agricultural innovation.

In conclusion, the Mayan civilization was such a highly developed civilization that it took a remarkable position among the ancient complex civilizations. The accuracy of their astronomical system, along with the complexity of their calendars, aesthetic refinement, unique architecture,
mathematical systems, and writing, were not surpassed by any civilization in the New World. Furthermore, they were matched by just a few in the Old World. Dispassionately, I can say that the Mayan culture was one of the great cultures of our planet. Gradually, these images were disappearing, and were taking in place of my life's memory since I can remember ... I cannot say they were anecdotes or specific parts of my life. They were kind of quick, or momentary. It seemed I could have clearly perceived colors, sounds, and even smells that were present back in their time. There seemed to be a broken time machine, back to the past. It was there, in a moment of my life, already lived. I could not see myself, but clearly saw my parents, uncles, cousins, childhood friends, and others. I listened to their conversations with each other, or me. In no time, my voice was heard, but their voices, their faces, all belonged to that era. I was in Cuba, and I could see my house, appeared as it was, with all its

details. If I tried to remember it later, it would have been very difficult to remember many details. I see myself running up and down the stairs, exactly as before. I could clearly see my room, my bed and other furniture. On a wall, on the back of my bed, was the shelf with my collection of boats and planes, handmade by me, some made of plastic, and the oldest made of gummed paper. A great joy filled me. I experience, living again, with the same objects around me. Suddenly, everything changed, and I was older. It was my time as a college student, and I was in a law school. I saw my classmates in university square, some walking; others in a group ... the trees were full of birds. It was morning, minutes before classes begin. Then I was walking down the street in my neighborhood. I saw cars parked on the street. Later, I found myself watching the sea from my room, which I did often because the ocean attracts me. I could see the waves filled up, and then break into pieces against the rocks of the jetty, with an impressive sound. The sky seemed to have a very bright blue, with a different salty breeze. Experienced safety and stillness in which I lived. I saw it all; with extraordinary clarity as if they were happening in front of me like a 3D color film. All my life seemed so insignificant compared to the greatness of the Mayan culture that, for a moment, I smiled against the contrast ... Then occupied my mind, images of my wife Maria Elena, my daughters, the new house, where I moved mentally. I could clearly see the building where I lived, and at the top, our apartment. It was night and watched the lights. I could clearly see my room, but now I felt as floating in one ceiling corner of it. Maria Elena was lying down in bed reading a magazine. Everything seemed quiet. I realized that what I was experiencing at that moment was real, current, and it was not an image of the past. I was there that night and in the same minute. Suddenly, the phone rang. The image and the noise went away, and I was back inside the tomb of Palenque. I do not think I would have fallen asleep. The darkness was absolute; it did not matter if my eyes were open or closed. I do not know if the ideas and images that came to my mind were the product of a dream in full consciousness, possibly overshadowed by the perception of such images, and the development of it or, did I travel in TIME? Is it possible? Isn't it? I realized that we were locked tightly by our daily lives. This creates a barrier that prevents us from understanding in capturing the messages left by other civilizations in its monuments and hieroglyphics ... It is as, at this time of my life, I would have approached the "Creator"... And when I speak of the "Creator", I do not mean the one of the Catholics or the Jews, nor of the Persians or the Arabs. I am referring to something above all this, in a philosophical and transcendent projection. I sat still, leaning on the triangular stone entrance to the tomb itself. I had lost track of time. The last time I saw my watch's luminous sphere, it showed one am after the luminosity of the sphere was completely overshadowed. When I had completed the process of thoughts and images I already described, I worried that it was daytime and could harm the custodian who let me in against the provisions. I decided to leave, but it was quite difficult because the darkness. Feeling the walls, I managed to find the stairs. I went, crouching to the leader inside the pyramid. Once there, I saw the outlet opening at the top of the pyramid, where a little sunshine entered, and went on all fours, feeling the wall, to the top. I looked at my watch, as the sky was beginning to clear, and saw the time: 5:50 a.m. After I reached the top, I went down the outside stairs to the ground. I walked two blocks to reach my rental car, and drove, 120 kilometers, to Villa Hermosa. At the airport, I returned the car, and boarded the plane that would take me to Mexico City. There, I would wait for the plane, from Miami, bringing my wife and starting a short vacation.

Physical Effects.

The force that holds the internal pyramid is, not connected to the outside. I performed my telepathy test using the cards with my wife and my friend Raul, who were both in Miami and in different, places, but I failed completely. None of them could receive a telepathic message from me, and neither me from them. However, there is a force in the pyramid that acts internally. Thus, the camera battery stopped working after a much shorter time period than usual, despite its being new. A curious fact, without explanation on my part is that, my body was charged with electricity the next few days after my departure from the pyramid. In that time I touched a metal object with my hands, and a spark jumped between my fingers and the object. The spark was intense, and at night, looked resplendent green, shaped bay. I could not touch the light switch in our hotel room, although, it is made of an insulating material. I had to switch it on with a wooden stick. Even my clothes bothered me because I felt the hairs on my body with electricity, rubbing on my clothes. Certainly, I had a nasty moment, when I was introduced to a high official of the Palace of Fine Arts of Mexico. When we shook hands, we receive strong electric shocks. My new friend was so puzzled that I had to give him some explanations, to ease the pain after it had passed. On the fourth day, we were quite concerned about the phenomenon. Both my wife and I, we tried everything we could think of, to neutralize the electricity. I bathe with cold water, hot water, with salt, with baking powder, wear clothing of different materials, but the phenomenon persisted. I was embarrassed to go out and enjoy my vacation. Until the fifth day when the electric charge disappeared completely, taking it away our major concern. Something in the pyramid act charged me with that electricity.

Paranormal effects.

In addition to these physical phenomena and mental experience under the pyramid, I experienced a change in my way of facing life. My attitude towards everything around me has changed, and I think I can face problems more safely, and in calm. Sometimes I think that if he had remained inside the pyramid, instead of a night, a week or a month, I would have changed completely. I would have left that pyramid a different man, a completely different person in character and thoughts. This feeling could be compared to what some of the first astronauts suffered after their returns to earth, some of them quit their jobs, left their homes and families, everything, and went preaching and writing books with a new philosophy about what is life. Travel through the cosmos and see the Earth as one brighter spot in the infinite space, made them feel how lowest is our daily lives, compared to the splendorous astral stage in which we live.

Concluding.

Michael Collins, Apollo II astronaut to the moon, in his book "Carrying the Fire" tells us: "Fly through space and see the Earth from afar, has changed my perception of things ... I feel different from other people ... my body molecules are different ... I tried to sort everything observed, though I could not fully understand ..."

Does the Palenque pyramid affect me the same way some astronauts were influenced on their space flight? What is the cosmic connection of the pyramids? What is the Mayan-Egyptian link in the construction of the pyramids? Why the Maya coincide with the Bible in the representation of the cross? How do the Mayan use the psychological and physical effects, experienced by me, inside the pyramid? Who teach them that? Does the low relief of the plate or slab closing the sarcophagus is a representation of an alien that visited the Earth, inside a spaceship, and died among the Mayas? Are the Palenque man, an extraterrestrial? Does the pyramid have an internal force?

To the last question, is the only one I can give an answer: I am convinced, that yes, the pyramid of Palenque, where I spent the night, has a not yet understood force by us Westerners...

Chapter Seven

Paranormal Experiences

Hynek's pipe

J. Allen Hynek was a scientist, astronomer, professor, and ufologist with fixed ideas and always enjoyed visiting Dr. Willy Smith, a scientist and ufologist. Hynek always occupied the same room they had prepared for the guests. The room consisted of two single beds, two bedside tables with their lamps, a small table and chair facing the window, and a chair or armchair.

When visitors left, Willy and his wife Terry were given the task of collecting and washing bedding, and moving all the pieces to clean the carpet with a vacuum cleaner. After this cleaning job, they set everything in place so that the room was ready for the next guest.

On his last visit, Hynek traveled directly to the hospital, and doctors discovered not only a prostate cancer, but also a brain tumor.

After his dead in 1986, many guests occupied that bedroom, including, me. I was there one weekend because I signed up for a course of professional molds making, near Willy's home.

Time passed, and at the end of 1990, I visited Willy and spent a weekend in the guest room, this time with my wife, Maria Elena. She could not sleep those nights, arguing that Hynek's presence was in the armchair. In the morning, she informed Smith of her feelings. Nonetheless, Willy argued that Hynek loved us and would be incapable of harming us much less frightening us.

The next night, the same thing happened. Maria Elena said she sensed Hynek's presence in the room, particularly in the armchair. To calm her down a little, we placed the beds together and left the lights on, but even so, she still could not sleep. In the morning, we informed Willy about what happened, and then we returned to Miami.

More time passed, and we had to go back up to a convention in Orlando near Willy's house. He, of course, he invited us to spend the night at his home, but Maria Elena flatly refused. Willy and Terry were quite upset, for a few minutes. However, they soon realized the reason and offered to take us to a nearby hotel. They would also have breakfast with us in the morning. During breakfast, the topic came up, and Willy, who was skeptical about all types of paranormal experiences, confessed that Hynek once promised him: "If there is something after death, I'll let you know." At the time, Willy thought Hynek was joking.

More time passed until one day, the phone rang. It was Willy. His voice crack with emotion and amazement: "Virgil, you do not know what happened to us. We were cleaning the room, after a guest left, and when we were moving the armchair for vacuuming the floor, we found the unmistakable Hynek's pipe. After Hynek's death, we cleaned and moved the furniture more than one hundred times. I have called you immediately because we remember the experiences of Maria Elena in the room."

"I am very confused, this is amazing!" Willy said.

Author with Hynek's pipe.

Comet Halley

Comet Halley, officially called 1P/Halley, is a large, bright comet that orbits the sun on average every 75-76 years. However, its orbital period can range between 74 and 79 years. It is one of the best known and brightest comets of "short period" Kuiper Belt. It was last seen in 1986 near the orbit of the Earth, and it is estimated to be its next perihelion in 2061. Although there are brighter comets than it, Halley is the only short-cycle comet that is visible to the naked eye; as a result, there are many references to its appearances, being the best documented. Source: Wikipedia.

Hynek pipe was not the only paranormal experience that he expressed in tone "joke". Hynek, on several occasions, had said jokingly: "He was born with Comet Halley and die when it returned." Thus, so it happened. Hynek was born on May 1, 1910 to the passageway of Halley's Comet and died at age 75, on April 27, 1986, exactly 75 years later during the arrival of the comet. Hynek had planned a trip to Mendoza, Argentina because he had wanted to see the return of the comet in the house of our friend Atilio Spinello, located in Potrerillo, Mendoza. By the way, when we were in that house, investigating the case of Ricardo in 1982, Hynek chose a living room sofa and refused to use any other room. Later, I asked Atilio: "Why did you left Hynek sleep on a couch?" To which, he replied: "The

sofa, in the living room, has a strong energy. That's where we do our prayers and meditations."
"Apparently Hynek felt the energy and did not want to be disturbed," said Atilio.

Hynek's encounter with Ashtar Sheran

This story happened on our first trip to a UFO conference by F.A.E.C.E, in Mendoza, Argentina, in 1980.

Upon arriving at the airport in Mendoza, and getting off the plane, we were greeted by local authorities and Faruk Allen, the event organizer. We went directly, without passing through customs, which was a surprise to Hynek, to a few cars that took us directly to the hotel. During the tour around the streets of Mendoza, we were escorted by two police motorcycles with sounding sirens. This caused another surprise to Hynek. He lowered the auto glass and almost went out, trying to take photos of the motorcade, but Faruk told him not to do it because we were passing through a military barracks and were prohibited to take photos there. Hynek said: "No one will believe me when I tell on."

We arrived at the hotel, and after settling, we were taken to a room where some groups were waiting to share their experiences with Hynek. I served as translator. A group told us that they can communicate with Commander, Ashtar Sheran, of the Cosmic Federation and if permitted, one of its members could be in mental contact with him. Hynek agreed, and during mental contact, Ashtar invited him to a meeting on a mountain.

When they left, I warned Hynek of the danger, that the group's director, Perla Edith Perviu, claimed to be descended from an Egyptian Princess and that she dressed in costumes of that time, all in white. A photo with her could put Hynek in a difficult position, in the eyes of other scientists. Nevertheless, he had already accepted the invitation and could not refuse.

On the next day, we were taken, by the congress organizers, to her house. Perla had invited us for a vegetarian dinner in preparation for the meeting with Ashtar. However, only one of the groups was allowed to enter the house with us. The rest stayed out on the street. Hynek asked her to at least let some of our group accompany us. If we did not do this, he would cancel the meeting. Now in a bad mood, Perla chose the one who would accompany us in his car.

After dinner, we rode in the car, with Hynek sitting next to the "Egyptian Princess" and me in front with the driver. On the way up the mountain, the automobile's lights blinked several times. Perla said it was caused by the energy of alien ships.

Finally, we reached the top of the mountain. The area was already prepared by the aliens as there were some large stones forming a circle. We all sat near one of them. The darkness was complete. All of the stars could be seen in the sky so clearly that it seemed as if we could touch them with our hands. As you might understand, Hynek was enjoying this view of the sky.

Meanwhile, the group initiates some praying, and the "Egyptian Princess" stands behind each one and slowly puts his hands on, but not touching, our heads.

Suddenly, someone said, "Look, over the horizon, is the ship of Ashtar Sheran." We all looked, and what we saw was a light, slowly rising in the horizon and starting to go bigger.

Hynek stopped, stared at the light, and said: "No, that's the planet Venus". Then a great light blinded us all. It was a powerful flashlight that our companion had. Hynek said: "We are leaving" and we went to our companion's car. On the way back, Hynek explained: "If you look to the horizon the thick layer of pollution's atmosphere creates an optical phenomenon of distortion to the very bright stars, in this case were Venus. If you wait and place Venus about 25 degrees high, this phenomenon disappears"

"It was an adventure, Hollywood style, I would never forget".

The last call.

One day, I hear that Hynek had been seriously ill and that his life was in danger. His death came very fast and took us by surprise.

His illness left him with no voice. He could not talk! The last conversation I had with him was during a call from his wife Mimi. She informed me that Hynek could not speak, but he wanted to know whether I had made arrangements for the trip to Mendoza? A few years ago, we had planned a trip to Mendoza to observe the Comet Halley.

For me, it was one of the hardest moments of my life, having to speak to him knowing that he could not answer me. Also, I was unable to show any feeling because we knew his health declined rapidly, and he was about to die. I felt a lump in my throat, and tears ran down my cheeks. I will never forget that moment.

A week later, Willy invited me to travel to visit Hynek, but I declined to go. I could not see him in those conditions. I preferred to remember him, as when we traveled together.

Wrapping up.

I brought up some of the anecdotes that occurred to scientists Hynek and Willy because I'm sure the same thing or something must have happened to others but that their positions have not been made public. I'm sure many have had some paranormal experiences or psychic abilities.

Chapter Eight

CUBAN SIGHTINGS

For some time past, UFO's in many guises had been sighted in the skies over the island of CUBA so called "The Key of the Caribbean" for its privileged position in the area. During the past 40 years, the communist government lead by Fidel Castro ignored and did not report any sightings over the island. Nevertheless, we are doing research, with Cuban exiles, and here we provide overviews of some unpublished sightings. We believe the information received should be noted by others investigators. The cases are offered here without evaluation.

1954. - Between Cuba and Florida.
Date: November. Time: 4:30 a.m.

Tacoma-class frigate Jose Marti.

Tacoma-class frigate Maximo Gomez.

Two frigates of Cuban Navy military, "José Martí"
and "Máximo Gómez", they were patrolling the
North coast of Cuba between the 4 to 6 miles of
the coast in front of the Matanzas Province. Its
destiny was the Havana bay. About the 4:30 in the
morning they began to observe intense lights in
the horizon. When something similar happens, the
deck officer must inform his commander of the
situation. The lights appeared by the northwest.
The frigates were put on alert. The lights came
near at a tremendous speed, and in seconds they
were over the ships. Three lights were forming a
V. The lights follow the frigates for four or six
minutes. Then, because the two frigates were
combated ready, most of the sailors were outside
watching the lights. The photographer, on board
of one of the ships, activated a 70 millimeter film
camera, and filmed the UFOs when they were
above of the ships, and followed the lights until,
moving slowly to the west, disappeared in the
horizon.

The film lasted from seven to ten minutes, and the
telephoto followed the UFOs until two miles in the

horizon. The film, in black and white, was of superior quality. In some frames, it was possible to observe the lights and the top structure of the frigates. The camera was located next to the cannon on the bow of one of the ships.

The UFOs maintained the same distance among them and the photographer had to swing the camera to film the three lights, and in the last frames, you can see the three lights, flying at slow speed, disappear in the horizon.

Ten days after the sighting, the film was shown to the Cuban military High Commands at the Cuban Navy building. Our witness was present and confirmed us that also the radar of the frigates detected the 3 objects when the UFOs appeared in the horizon until they disappeared to the west.

An expert, analyzing the film, declared that a physical object could be seen inside the intense lights. This created a great impact between the presents. The film was sent, in a Navy airplane, to the U.S. Navy Intelligence in Key West, Florida.

Most of the Cuban high ranking officials are now living in Florida, and they wish to maintain its anonymity. This report is based on interviews to officials and sailors who were eyewitnesses.

FALSE UFO. 1954. Havana.
NOTE: I was a teenager when, on television, I saw a live broadcast, of a flying saucer parked in the middle of a famous square. This left me very impressed. It was the first time I learn about "Flying Saucers".

The city of Havana was impacted with excitement to publicize, the Day of the Innocents (April fools) which compared to what was the source of the Via Blanca, now Revolution Square, in Rancho Boyero's Road, had landed a large Flying Saucer. It was calculated; between fifteen and twenty thousand people show up, early in the morning, to that place, when they learn that the landing of a Flying Saucer, was broadcasted alive, on television. Habaneros lived hours of emotional intensity. Many arrived from all parts of the island; others were locked in their homes for fear of the unknown.

From six in the morning until eleven at night, the Rancho Boyero Road's traffic was disrupting, due to the number of people that wanted to see the Flying Saucer. Police, firefighters and military members rushed to the scene in a spectacular show of force trying to keep order.

When someone approached the UFO, it blows a white smock, with strange sounds, turning on colored flashing lights on its edge.

Late at night, the police stomp the UFO plasterboard, and out came five "Aliens", which turned out to be television stars, with toy laser gun. The five "Aliens" were arrested, and then released by police, because it was not been notified of the publicity stunt for a TV program "My Favorite Husband", and "La Tropical" beer company.

el platillo de la habana 1954

The five " Aliens", that came out of the disc were;
Rogelio Hernández, Armando Bianchi, Marta
Velez, Herminia de la Fuente, and Rosita Fornes
(seen here, in the photo, taking off the helmet of
interplanetary travel). It was the most sensational
April Fool's Havana remembers!
Source: Bohemia magazine, and Diario de la
Marina, Wednesday, December 24, 1954

1957. - Oriente Province. Bacuranao.
Time: 4.a.m. Date: Winter.
Two sport fishermen, Raul and Luis, observed "a
huge and brilliant UFO, color white-pink", to come
to the surface of the sea creating a white surf
waves. The UFO illuminated the clouds, flying

over the witnesses' yacht and creating an "artificial rain" with the dripped drops of salt water.

1957.- Oriente Province. Guantanamo.
Time: 9 p.m. Date: December. A detachment of government soldiers lead by Captain Fermin Fernandez, Lieutenant Pablo Rosa and Lieutenant Jose Tamargo, observed a yellow light coming down the sky became a huge silver disc, that landed a short distant from them. Overwhelmed by the sighting, the soldiers retreated. The three officers made a half circle and opened crossfire with their machine guns (45 Caliber Thompsons). Amusingly, the bullets never hit the metal structure. "There was a zone that repelled the bullets". The UFO began glowing yellow, speeded up and disappeared into the sky.

1880. - Camaguey Province.
In a State Government Farm named "Kilo 7".
Date: April 16, Time: 10 pm.
Some political prisoners observed a large blue light high in the sky. A smaller light came out of the large one and hovered about two blocks from the witness. Later on, it went up and fused with the large light. The witness went to the place where the UFO had hovered close to the ground, and found tropical fruits: big oranges, papayas and apples (Cuba does not produce apples, and many of the witness did not know what there were). Pablo, one of the witnesses, claims that his gangrened leg healed after he ate the fruits.

OCTOBER 1995.

A big "wave" of UFO sightings was reported across the island of Cuba. We received reports, almost daily. Many of them, from witnesses arrived in Miami from the island. Here are some of them:

The Cuban official radio reported that, during the first week of October, they received daily reports of UFOs flying over the island. In Puerto Padre, Las Tunas, at 10:00 PM, a lady (not identified) reported seeing a UFO, with a very bright light. She also said that she had seen several UFOs before, but not as clear as on this occasion. 'Several people saw it' she said. "At first, we thought it was an airplane, but there was no sound. The object was moving up, down, and sideways. Then passed low over the village and disappeared into the city of Holguin". The day before, also in the city of Santi Spiritu, and at the same time, 10:00 pm, there were more sightings. In Majibacoa and in Calixto Garcia town, in the province of Holguin, a group of officers, standing on guard that night, reported the presence of a bright light in the sky. At first, they thought it was a helicopter, but the light flew and disappeared at high speed. Other cases were reported, several days later, in the city of Havana, in San Antonio de los Baños, and three in Florida, in the eastern province of Camaguey.

NOTE: This was the first time in 37 years that the Cuban government openly acknowledged the existence of UFOs, with news from the official government Radio Rebelde, to the Cubans living on the island. That surprised us. We never expect it. Why did the government wait so long? We don't know. Most of the reports, we were collecting of this wave, come from people fleeing the island

1995. Near the town of Torriente.
Province of Matanzas.
Date: October 15, Time: 9: a.m.
In October of 1995, the Sunday newspaper Juventud Rebelde published an article about this case.

The article stated, "Perhaps, Adolfo Zarate's biggest fear was that what happened to his cousin Ricardo Zarate, would happen to him. His cousin disappeared two years earlier, in 1993, after leaving his house early in the morning to work in a farm. The search for Ricardo lasted more than a month until the case was closed. Until this day, his disappearance is still unexplained.

Perhaps because of that reason, the rain, the loneliness of that Sunday, and most certainly, because of the strange looking sphere that was descending from the sky and landed only 60 meters away from him, Adolfo decided to hide among the corn crops. He could have gotten closer to the object, but the fear of being abducted and never returned like his cousin prevented him from doing so. According to him, the machine stood still after landing. Moments later, an individual that appeared to be wearing a gas mask and camouflaged clothes came out of it. The ship also had a type of camouflage because it resembled the same colors as the crops. As it started to rain even harder, the individual walked around the ship and later leaned on the door to talk to yet another one inside the cockpit. He appeared to be picking up plants from the field. Later, he climbed up the stairs and the machine emitted a bright blue light. Adolfo felt a tremendous air pressure as the ship left.

The newspaper Juventud Rebelde also published Adolfo's own words. He stated, "It was the same size of an amusement ride found at the fairgrounds. I could not tell what it was made of. It did not have wings, propellers, nor did it make any noise. It had an oval shape. It landed on two legs that appeared to have some type of air shocks. It also appeared to have very small wheels because it left wheel tracks behind. I could not see the individual's face, but he appeared to be an ordinary human being. The individual did not appear to be carrying any weapons".

A commission of scientists was formed to investigate the case. Unfortunately, they did not come up with any conclusions. Nevertheless, they did conclude that Adolfo Zarate was mentally sane and determined that he had good credibility. Dr. Oscar Alvarez Palomares, a physics, mathematician, and chief astronomer of the Cuban Astronomy and Geophysics Department, personally gave me his opinion about this case. "Although Zarate is a respected farmer, his knowledge regarding these types of phenomena is very limited; therefore, I do not have enough evidence to tell you whether it was indeed a craft nor that it was not. Additionally, I could not find anything out of the ordinary where this event allegedly took place", he said.

It had passed nearly a week after the event by the time we arrived. It simply comes down to whether the testimony of that person is valid or not. Furthermore, it's only one eyewitness. Nevertheless, the event took place at a short distance of 200 meters from one of the nation's major highways and during broad daylight.

We could not resolve the case. There was no additional evidence. There were no other reports. After 6 or 7 days since the incident, there were no longer tracks or marks that would point out that any unknown object had been there at all. Moreover, there were no signs of burns on the ground or in the grass. Zarate himself told us that he was in good health, even a year later, when we decided to visit him and see if anything unusual had happened ever since. Science it's always based on facts; It takes into account reports, records, and irrefutable evidence; therefore, it does not allow any room for doubts or imperfections. Given the fact that we could not find any evidence, we registered our investigation as "personal curiosity". However, we had the opportunity to interview Cuban ufologist Orestes Girbau Collado. In addition to his 34 years of experience investigating UFO phenomena, he's also a meteorologist at the Matanzas weather station.

Collado stated, "Something did land in that area and I'm almost 100% sure that it wasn't from our planet. I'm not just coming to this conclusion because the radar did not pick up any contacts. As a professional meteorologist, I can assure that, during that day, we had several cloud formations. Some of the characteristics of the clouds were typical of most rainy days. Some of the formations were at high altitudes, and some at low altitudes. The ship was not from our origin; it came either from a different dimension, time or planet, but I don't know exactly. During that year, there were similar other sightings and landings like this one throughout Spain, Chile, Peru, Argentina, Colombia and many other Latin American countries. There were even reports of appearances by humanoids in Spain, which may mean that the amount of record numbers of sightings were at their peak. One of the reasons why I don't believe that it was an aircraft was the rainy weather itself and the awkward place where it landed. Furthermore, there's no way that it was an advanced aviation craft, such as a spy plane, simply because they use satellite heat censoring tracking systems. Because they can't use radar, they have to rely on satellites to track their heat signature to report and verify their position. The weather presented very harsh conditions to

 conduct these types of operations".

What about the rice ears?

"The situation with rice ears came later because they got crushed; nevertheless, some time later some colleagues went there, and they found that in the surrounding areas, some small rice ears with "black tips" grew around, that is to say that they grew on their own, or spontaneously because they were in a place nobody planted them. Although Zarate suffered some rare symptoms, such as swollen and watery eyes, during that time, he did not notice anything unusual with that; however, those are typical characteristics of UFO landings. Those effects are caused by the fuel or by the EMP waves found during high combustion transfers or perhaps a physical-chemical effect that UFOs create. Until recently, Zarate still had those symptoms.

Zarate is a person with very little imagination; he did not know anything about UFOs. In fact, he knew about them as much as I know about old Hebrew languages, which I know nothing about. Furthermore, I think he was fearful of talking about it. He probably thought that it was some kind of espionage operation, and he did not want to be subject to intense questionings. I also think that Zarate was very lucky because if it weren't for the corn crops nearby, he would not have had the chance to hide. If he had been walking along the open field - if I can speculate bit-, he would have been gone just like his cousin who disappeared two years earlier during the same date, the same crop field, at around the same time. This sounds incredible but is true".

During the summer of 1999, a program was broadcasted on Cuban television; it was a documentary called UFOs in Cuba. It was done by Hugo Parrado, Armando Linares and Octavio Cortazar. Upon asking Cortazar his opinion about Zarate case, he stated: "We knew Zarate, we knew the place where he saw the ship and the aliens, because evidently what he saw, in my opinion, was an extraterrestrial ship and what came out of it were indeed aliens. What's most amazing is that Zarate presents the typical characteristics of the person that has had extraterrestrial contact. Furthermore, I was astonished with what happened with the ground at the place of landing; the soil used to be fertile. Now, no plant can grow in that spot, which again, is very typical on most UFO landing spots. Even Zarate himself has tried using many different types of plants and fertilizers without any success. This was the same soil that only days before the landing, he was able to grow his crops from. He still does not understand how fertile soil can suddenly turn into dry useless ground. With regards to the effects caused to his body, I'm convinced that these physical symptoms are typical of people who have contact with this unknown craft. It was most certainly caused by his proximity to the ship".

DECEMBER, 1995.
A wire agency EFE reported a UFO sighting in Guara, a small town south of Havana, the cable said that a UFO landed and out came three entities, collected boil and left taking some people. With the cooperation of the local radio station WQBA, we made telephone contact with witnesses in Melena del Sur, a town near Guara. We interviewed Dr. Mercedes Alcazar M.D, of 45 years of age, who informed us that, on the night of December 13, between 7:00 and 7:30 PM, they saw a UFO.

"It looked like a bus, with many bright lights turning one after the other. We could not calculate how height it, but it seemed very high. You could distinguish it as a big ball of lights. If was something different, of what we used see at night. It had an incandescent glow. "Carlos Borroto, 13-year- old son of Dr. Alcazar told us: "It was very strange. It did not look like an airplane. It had many yellow lights on, as small bulbs. It was like a star -shaped snacks. At first the object was moving slowly, but suddenly it fell, and hit the ground. Then, it went up and rapidly disappearing. I did not felt fear, but I was impressed, because I had never seen anything like it. Here in town, it was like a bomb. The militants ran with their guns to the cane field, where the UFO touched down. The UFO mobilized the entire village. Everyone ran to the cane field, some cycling. But when they arrived, the UFO was gone". We asked him. Did you see any entities inside the UFO? And, if the UFO took with them any people? To which, he answered: "I have not heard anything about that, to me; that's a lie. I was with my mom and two aunts talking in the garden when the UFO appeared. My aunts also saw it. "Again, we went to phone Dr. Alcazar and told us: "Here the authorities have not given any explanation. Absolutely nothing". She told us: "I wish that the UFO would have collected all us, and taken us there! (To Miami)" With this expression, we decided to cut the telephone interview.

APRIL, 2002
On the outskirts of Sancti Spiritus city, Camaguey province.

In April, 2002, Damaso Gonzales Salas had his first encounter with a UFO, when, at night, it landed, close to his home, in his ranch. Damaso witness the landing. Tacking his battery operated fluorescing lantern, walk toward the UFO.

213

When he was a few feet from the craft, he stops and looks at it for detail. The UFO was about 30 meters around, without windows or portholes, and it looks metal-silver. Then, he tries to contact it, turning on and off his lantern. A ray of light, from the UFO, hit his lantern, turning it off. Later, he was unable to fix it. Then, the UFO, slowly, at first, took off, and then, at high speed disappeared to the north.

On Wednesday, March 5, 2003, about 10 o'clock, Damaso Gonzalez Salas and his wife went to sleep. Damaso wake up at a strange noise, and a horse neighing at the back of his home. Checking his watch, it was past five o'clock in the morning.

He went outside to see what was happening. When he reaches the back of his home, he watches a bright circular light. He when close to it, without fear, an encounter two entities similar to human beings. He described them to be thin, white skin, one was blond, and the other has dark hair. They ware green long leaves overalls with turtle necks. These entities, gesturing with their hands, invite him to a landed UFO. A door opened under the UFO, and small steps went down. Damaso went up inside, and the two entities stay outside. He enters a small room; its walls were cover by glasses or dark mirrors. In the center of the room was a chair. He seat, and start looking around him. He saw, like a plate with strange symbols and number, from 9 to 0.

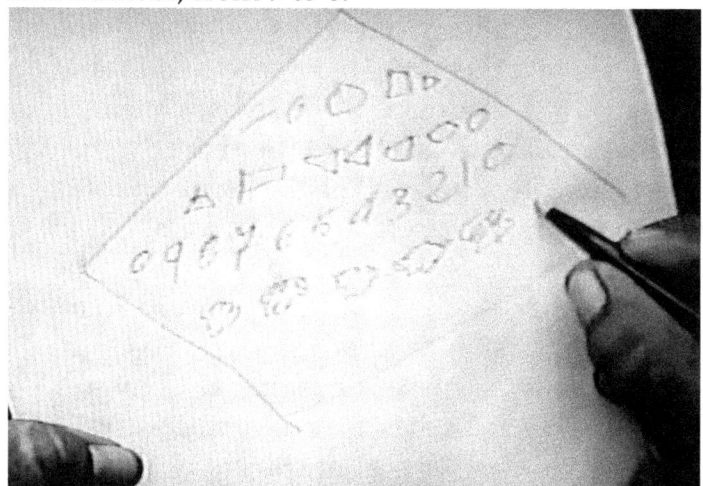

Later on, he heard a sound, like air pressure and saw small lights inside the wall glasses. Now he could see outside, and fill fear when he sees the stars passing fast in the sky. After a few minutes, the speed slow down, and a door open. The two entities was, already outside, and invited him to step out. He could not identify where he was. The ground looks like bright sand. He bent and took a hand full of it, but one entity touch his hand signaling him to throw it, but he was able to save a little in his short pockets. Again, the two entities invited him to step inside the UFO. This time, beside the stars, he could see the sea. Them, one of the entities put his fingers tips in Damaso forehead, at that moment, he started feeling weak, cold and sleeping. When he woke up, he was laid down in a grass next to a street. In a building, next to him, were two men and a woman. He asks them, where he was, and the time. They answer that he was in front of the Guatemala embassy, and the time was five minutes to six o'clock in the morning. He told them was happened to him, and was taken for a madman. Damaso asks them to call the police. The police took him to the 8 Police Station. There, he repeats his history, and the police too, think he was crazy. After several call to his home in Sancti Spiritus, the police verify the story, and change their attitude toward him, offering a pair of shoes and a T-shirt. Damaso still fell sick and was taken to a hospital at Columbia Military base. After a basic medical checkup, he was an interview by several intelligent officers. A lieutenant colonel took the "sand" from his shorts for analysis. Finally, they ask him what type of transport he likes to go back to his home, and he answer, by train.

216

Damaso's wife declares; Damaso went out, without shoes and shirt, and did not return, she calls him about 5:30 a.m. She saw a strong light in the sky but did not associate it with Damaso. After, looking for him, she went to the police and reports him as a "missing person". Damaso dies in April 2006.

Photos by Carlos Heredero.

The Light of YARA

UFO sightings report always occurred in the western part of the island. For all its peculiarity, Cubans call it "The Light of Yara". I have personally interviewed many of these witnesses. This phenomenon has been seen by thousands of witnesses and dates from pre-Columbian times. It all started with a myth.

The Legend.

Many witness the death of the Indian cacique. Hatuey, who arrived in Cuba to lead a rebellion against the Spanish colonizers. Before, he had survived an attack by the Spanish army led by Diego Velázquez, with a group of five Indian chiefs, in the Island Espanola, which is today called the Dominican Republic.

Four of them perished, when the house, where they were meeting, was burned by the Spaniards. However, one managed to escape; Hatuey. His leadership qualities have been visible to the suspicion of Velázquez. Aware of the danger, and what this meant about the intentions of the conquerors, Velazquez decided to follow him to Cuba, where after capture, in the small town of Yara, condemned him to burn at the stake, as an example to the rest of the Indians.

It was said, by those who saw the huge fire that a light came out from the flames, and it was the soul of Hatuey, wandering and waiting for the time of eternal revenge. Thus was born the legend of "La Luz de Yara".

Many witnesses maintain to see it up until now, in the north part of the eastern provinces. Sometimes, they say, it is accompanied by a strong wind, and then divided in several parts of different colors; it began to jump, as if it were playing, and then rejoined, and went the way it came, either from the top of the mountains, or the deep waters of the sea. Fishermens say, that when the light appears, the fish do not bite, so they have to stop fishing, and wait for the light to go away.

Testimonies.

"The red light is full, and shines", declares a witness. "It comes over the sea; I have seen it. Its reflection can be seen in the water and is very bright."

"It came out from under a hill, "says another," or from the crest of a mountain. It divided into two or three parts, and went bond, you can see a big flash."

"I've seen it several times," adds another. "Split into three equal parts of different colors: yellow, blue, and green. I'm a fisherman, and once, while, on a fishing boat, it was so close, I had a lot of fear. It lights up the coast.".

Some are said, to have been paralyzed by the light while others claim that they have seen a human figure, or humanoid. "I saw it", said a neighbor in the area, "It was red as a lantern. It started on the plateau, and went flying and hovering in the sea ... then went to the beach and ran to the reefs. Sometimes you can see, inside the light, a man. I saw it too, so I say."

Officials.

In the beginning of Communist rule, on the island of Cuba (1959), the authorities tried to shutdown the light, thus eliminating the religious aspect, symbolizing spiritual pilgrimage, and avoid, drawing believers and curious public, to the area. The first thing they tried, was to send two combat craft to the mountain where the light appeared. They spent several days shooting with cannons and machine guns. Unable to remove the light, they dynamited the mountain. After destroying part of the mountain, the light continued to appear in the top of it. Then decided it was incorrigible, and concentrated on threatening the people that come to see the light.

Other witnesses.

1. – On the night of September 1958, the first nuclear-powered aircraft carrier of the U.S. Navy, the USS Franklin D. Roosevelt, sailed, off the east coast of the island of Cuba, near Guantanamo Bay. On deck, Chester Grusinski and other sailors observed a white light near the ship:

"We noticed a small light that approached us. The light was increasing in its size and brightness. It passed so close, we could see its spherical shape, with windows, and even could see non-human figures inside as we were observed. The impression I got is that those figures were not human beings. The light approached, changed its color from white to red orange, and I could feel the heat on my face. It was spherical, in shape, with a size of about 75-100 feet. Its bottom was round and red. Then the object was gone. The entire sighting lasted some minutes."

2. - In the last days of October 1969, the U.S. DLG - 27 destroyer sailed from Guantanamo Bay along the coast of Cuba. It was nearly twelve o'clock when the crew saw suddenly, rising on

the horizon, a hard, shiny, silver object, like the moon. However, the object was a thousand times greater than the moon and continued there for about fifteen minutes. Back to base, the crew refused to report what they saw so that no one was going to make fun of them. It was not until the year 1974 that the crew decided to communicate what they saw. Reference: Enigma! Magazine No. 6, p. 5 "Mysteries in the Caribbean Seas."

3. - In April 1998, a navy officer walking on a long pier on Guantanamo Bay sighted bright lights underwater. "At first it was a bright white light moving very fast under the sea. Behind that light came two more, forming a sort of triangle, changing color to a bright red. It could measure about 10 feet in diameter. Each had a dome, but do not think that all three had the same measures. It was like 30 meters from the pier, and I was in the middle of it. They were moving very fast, and sometimes very slow, but always with a circular motion. I could see the lights as the light of day. I stopped walking and looked at them. I felt fear. I could not believe what I was seeing. Others sailors approached the dock, and I yelled for them to witness what was happening, but when they approached, the lights were gone. Still, I don't know what it was. Some told me that they could be trained dolphins, but no dolphins could move so fast, I repeat, very fast. Such lights were not made by

man. I served for 16 years in the Navy, and I've never seen anything like this. It was a chilling experience I'll never forget." Reference: Documentary USE. (Unidentify Submarine Object - Unidentified Submarine Object) "Deep Sea UFOs" Red Alert, History Channel TV.

Although Cuban authorities are trying to silence the phenomenon of La Luz de Yara, witnesses in that area, arriving to Miami, report that the lights continue to appear today.

We hope that, in a democratic future on the island, we can further investigate the phenomenon of La Luz de YARA.

Addendum

THE ROOTS OF COMPLACENCY

by J. Allen Hynek

Introduction

Toward the end of his life, Dr. J. Allen Hynek was a frequent visitor to my home, the last of such visits taking place from August 20 to August 31. 1985, when he finally left to have his first surgery on September 5, 1985. After that, his health declined rapidly and unfortunately he died on April 27, 1986.

During his visits, Dr. Hynek did quite a bit of work using my computer which was quite similar to his own at home. At that time, his interest was centered on the Hudson Valley sightings

Time marched on, and after Dr. Hynek passed away, the work was completed by Bob Pratt and published in book form in 1987, under the tittle NIGHT SIEGE.

One day, revising my diskettes, I found a file labeled "Imbrogno" which I did not recognize, When I opened it, it was a paper intended to be the Preface of the book that undoubtedly by error Allen had saved on one of my diskettes (on August 30, 1985, just the day before he left my home). It is a remarkable piece, and once you read it will be easy to understand why it was not used

223

as initially intended. I think the time has come to release it through the INTERNET. so everyone will see what Dr. Hynek's thoughts about these remarkable sightings really were. I strongly suggest that you compare "THE ROOTS OF COMPLACENCY" (as Hynek himself titled it) with the version that appeared in NIGHT SIEGE.

Dr. Willy Smith
UNICAT PROJECT
June 1999

Something truly astonishing happened.... Not far from New York City, along the Hudson Valley, as hundreds of astonished people looked up, many driving along the Taconic Parkway, they saw something no one had ever seen before.
Some called it a "Space-ship from outer space" (for want of anything better) but it was generally described by numbers of competent, professional persons as startlingly brilliant lights, in the form of a "V", or Boomerang, silent, slowly-moving, and very large close-by object. It has often popularly been called the "Westchester (County) Boomerang".

The world has never known about this, even though the event happened not once but several times, and over the course of several years. To all intents and purposes, this was a non-event. The media across the world have remained dumb.

Local papers, radios and TV's, it is true, did momentarily carry spots along with the daily news, but there the news just vanished.

How is it possible that in the United States, where even trivial events are often flashed across the world, only one TV and radio network carried an account of this utterly astounding event? Far, far lesser stories are spewed forth across the world!

Could it possibly be that the whole thing just never happened? No, many times there was good, but extremely local, media coverage; many hundreds have personally attested to us, and to many others that the "Westchester Boomerang" was most undeniably, very truly real to them. Furthermore, many witnesses at a given time, were geographically separate, and unknown to each other. Cars along the Taconic Parkway, a well traveled highway, stopped, and passengers looked in amazement, many frightened and bewildered at the spectacle.

Police department "blotters" proved that many calls came to several local police stations, and we have tape recordings of a number of the police involved. The Boomerang was undeniably real; it was not a chimera!

Yes, something truly and astonishing transpired, but was no one "minding the store", was everyone asleep at the switch? What about law enforcement agencies (whose duty is certainly to alert and assist when something amazing is afoot; what about civilian and military personnel?

When hundreds of largely professional, affluent people, in suburban areas, are astonished, awestruck, and many frightened by what they could only regard as a very bizarre event would this not at least warrant and bring forth some comment from the nation's media? And what about law officers, government officials and... what of the FAA which supposedly monitors the airwaves over which the "Boomerang" repeatedly flew, and thus constituted serious hazards, especially over the Taconic Parkway.

And what of scientists, to whom these events should have been of breathtaking scientific concern? But nothing...except, oh yes, a writer so inept at his task that not once did he checked, even briefly, the voluminous tapes and other material amassed by the present authors: a remarkable example of investigative reporting.

His conclusion: the Boomerang was caused by nothing more than a flight of small planes flying in formation, a totally untenable conclusion in view of the facts.

How, it would appear that we really have TWO astounding stories, rather than just one... different but related... and equally incomprehensible: the story of the low-flying luminous Boomerang (in itself which could rank high in the annals of science fiction... if it were science fiction!) and the second, a totally unaccountable dereliction of duty (and there seem to be no other word for it), a complete superb and indifference to accountability.

It was a malady which appeared to plunge all who encountered it, EXCEPT the witnesses, into a deadly stupor. Such a malady, or perhaps a virulent virus of apathy and indifference to duty, could immobilize cities and a whole country. Of course, we don't know what the Boomerang was really about for:

---the Police and other law enforcement officers were derelict and failed in their duty to assist the many who called for fear and danger, as well as in awe and wonder.

---the FAA utterly failed to be concerned for air safety, flight rules, navigation lights, when told that some utterly strange and possibly menacing object was cruising close over streets and house.

---the Military was derelict by not attending to public safety and matters of National Defense (the country could have been subtlety invaded!)

---the Scientists failed to uphold their "Hippocratic" oath of science: they were derelict in following the quest in following an outstanding mystery.

---the media, well, where were they? Truly derelict always avid news hounds, rushing to their typewriters or microphones to rush the news to the world (good, bad and trivial), but where were they? Hardly any of the 50 States heard the Boomerang story.

Why? Utterly indifferent and apathetic? If so, why?

Of the two stories, that of the Boomerang if by far the more directly told. Bizarre and fantastic though it may be (and is) it merely need competent retelling. The facts are on record. From hundreds of cassette tapes in thousands of statements made by witnesses, the Boomerang is a matter of record. But the second story, well, that is another matter.

This story is not at all directly told. Here, there are no cassette tapes, no clear cut descriptions, and no policeman, no scientist, no military man, no media person; no FAA has recorded why they were derelict. We can only infer as one might infer from the pages of history. We can only deduce and play detective. And we must try, for this second story, more truly a puzzle, could be of utmost importance to finding out how we, as humans, act under stress, trauma and fear..... For the Boomerang had all of these!

The puzzle has far more parts than the tale of the Boomerang. It is, indeed, a part of a continuing story of mankind's pioneering search for adventure and meeting, but repeatedly dashed and frustrated by those who cannot look to the heights of the pioneer: by the "it will never fly" or "it can't be done" mentalities. These who always must say "since it can't be done, there is no need to even thinking about it or even talking about it.

Therein lies the spawning ground of indifference, of apathy, and to dereliction of duty.

All those who didn't follow through on the Boomerang event were not willfully derelict: they were merely the thousands of "it will never fly" and "it can't be done" and so there is no need to think about it. The corollary is: "Since it can't be done, whatever said had been done, were simply deluded... they must have been mistaken, and so no need to look into it further". It is the failure to seek for the light of the tunnel because there could't be a light.

Intellectual adventure is sterile when there is continual inability to seek an answer to challenges, to seek ways out of the tunnel of indifference. In the story of the Boomerang, the FAA, the media, scientists, politicians, the military.... all may momentarily touch upon the mystery, but suddenly it appeared that apathy saps further energy to incentive, and in its stead is a great desire nothing... it becomes a hotbed of inertia... a great desire to do nothing, fobbing it all off in the guise of a handy solution, like "planes in formation".

It is not as from a seeming direct desire to be in duty, but it is more as though the call for duty has vanished, or as though some bad fairy had administered a sleeping potion, an apathy draught.

How else might one hold that otherwise responsible law enforcement, FAA, military, the media etc. would renege on their duties?

There is a more realistic answer than calling upon some bad fairy (though it would certainly fit the facts), and that is that it all lies in our human (mental) nature. A psychologist would express it more professionally, but it simply amounts to the fact that the human mind has definite limits for acceptance and accountability. In the history of science, this syndrome has been seen many times and in many ages. For instance, how often has it occurred that totally revolutionary ideas, as novel at first as to be utterly neglected or discarded... a form of apathy and total indifference.

As a homely analogy, one might say that such a totally novel idea "overheats the mental human circuits" and the fuse blow (or the circuit-breaker cuts out) as a protective device for the mind. The time is not yet right for the age and the new idea might just as well not been there in the first place. Mankind was not yet able to handle it.

Thus, when mankind is presented with a totally bizarre, shocking, traumatic event (the Boomerang?) a mental circuit cuts out. Instead of a challenge for action, there is a dead battery. This is, of course, well known in individual cases of amnesia in, for example, "shell shock": could it be that a collective amnesia or apathy can come into play? If so, might it be possible that collectively people can react traumatically, as to the Westchester Boornerang, to a collective amnesia, whether they are policemen, media people, the FAA etc.?

Whatever be the case, the effect is real. Many instances in history.... and the Boomerang are its most recent and spectacular example... when the breaking point of the collective mind occurs, it must openly disregard patent evidence of the senses: it can no longer encompass them within their normal borders.

The Holocaust perpetrated by Hitler in WW II is another sample: people simply refused to accept, and were indifferent to the evidence, because their minds couldn't bring themselves to accept that such a Holocaust could possibly be despite ample evidence. It was also a "mental circuit breaker" a general apathy and a will to indifference.

The Boomerang and the Holocaust are but striking samples of what happens when the collective mind willfully disregards evidence when "it can't take it". The entire modern UFO syndrome is another: here we have utterly ample evidence of the global nature of the UFO phenomenon. Thousands of instances and over many countries the evidence for the UFO phenomenon is clear, but those in position of policy and authority (FAA, educators, scientists etc) are deaf or purposely obtuse. Apathy goes hand in hand with the ability to accept even the most inane answers, anything whatever, just to stave off the necessity to think.

So we cannot at the moment expect to do little about the wealth of material collected on the Westchester Boomerang (or for the much more abundant wealth of UFO material). The circuits are closed; apathy holds sway. But history has shown that in time information and questions dam breaks, sometimes cataclysmically, and later, why, low and behold, the pundits by a complete irrational turn of fact, will say, "oh, we knew this all the time!".

Editor's note:

As detailed in NIGHT SIEGE, the first incident was reported on December 31, 1982, and the sightings continued until the date of publication of the book, with a concentration of incidents during the summer of 1984.